From EDEN to SAHARA

FLORIDA'S TRAGEDY

John Kunkel Small

New Forewords by Bill Belleville, Randy Mejeur, and Jay Exum

Published by the Seminole Soil & Water Conservation District
Sanford, Florida ◆ www.sswbc.org

From Eden to Sahara: Florida's Tragedy
by John Kunkel Small
Forewords by Bill Belleville, Randy Mejeur, and Jay Exum

Published by Seminole Soil and Water Conservation District
222 East 1st Street, Sanford, Florida 32771
www.sswbc.org

Cover design by Michelle Martin

Library of Congress Control Number: 2004111760

International Standard Book Number: 0-9761215-0-6

04 05 06 07 08- 987654321

Printed in the United States of America

Acknowledgements

Our greatest thanks to those selfless businesses and organizations that have generously funded the publishing of this book, and thus, have made the revitalization of *Eden to Sahara* a reality. Those underwriters include: Stenstrom, McIntosh, Colbert, Whigham, Reischmann & Partlow, P. A. (Sanford, Fla.), Colbert-Cameron Mitigation Bank (Sanford, Fla.), NaTeRe USA, Inc. (Sanford, Fla.), Environmental Management and Design, Inc. (Orlando, Fla.), North Lake Jesup Community, Inc. (Sanford, Fla.), Seminole Audubon Society (Sanford, Fla.), and a company which wishes to remain anonymous. We could not have published this book without your financial support.

At Seminole Soil and Water Conservation District (SSWCD), we are grateful for the individual elected board members who have encouraged our efforts. They include W. Steven Edmonds, Jr., Danny DeCiryan, William Clifford, Leslee Berryman, and Michael Barr. Thanks also to our attorney, Joe Rosier, esq., and Carol Johnson from the Florida Department of Agriculture who have thoughtfully supported this project.

The genesis for this publishing mission was born when Dr. Henry O. Whittier, former director of the University of Central Florida's Arboretum, first helped me understand the significance of Dr. Small's prophetic and important book. When I tried to track it down through various lending libraries, I found it to be a nearly impossible task. It was scarce for a good reason—it had been out of print since its first modest issuance in 1929 by the Science Press of Lancaster, Penna. Mike Barr, Chair of SSWCD, went to work trying to find a first-edition copy, and thanks to his tenaciousness, he finally succeeded. But the difficulty of locating a used copy of the book made him realize how rare it was, and it gave him an idea: Why not republish *From Eden to Sahara* and thus make it more widely available? We discussed the idea and agreed that bringing this important text back to print was especially vital given the growing concerns for the conservation of our unique landscape in this fast-growing state. What better goal for an agency with the mission of the conservation of soil and water?

Mike and I solicited Florida environmental author Bill Belleville to write a foreword to update the edition. Bill's own passion and skills helped take the project to an entirely new dimension. He urged us to use as many professionals as possible to help make this new version of *Eden to Sahara* the best book it could be, and offered to help facilitate that process. In doing so, Bill functioned as the de facto editor-publisher. He engaged Jay Exum and Randy Mejeur, two esteemed scientists with an environmental consulting firm in Orlando, to contribute a scientific foreword that placed Small's work into a modern perspective. Jay and Randy also assembled a complex annotated glossary of scientific terms to make it easier for the reader to cross-reference many of the author's original descriptions.

Bill then enlisted two others whose generosity, skills, and dedication added immeasurably to the final product and dramatically enhanced the way the book looked and read: Michelle Martin, an award-winning graphics designer at AAA headquarters in Heathrow, Fla., and Virginia Maxwell, an editorial project manager at a publishing house in central Florida. Both are as committed to professional standards as they are to the philosophy of a sustainable natural Florida. SSWCD volunteers Christine Bradbury and Nikita Spaulding went to work keying in the new text from the hard copy of the original book. Bill's friend and paddling buddy Robert Boswell, an Orlando area cardiologist with an abiding love of nature photography, provided the stunning cover image of a hammock of sabal palms from the lower Econlockhatchee River.

All of the contributors did so with no remuneration—other than to satisfy an abiding belief in the power of information to help readers more fully understand and connect with our natural world here in Florida. Thanks to all of you from the bottom of my heart.

Michelle Thatcher, Executive Director
Seminole Soil & Water Conservation District, Sanford, Fla.
2004

Contents

Prologue

I went down to Rock Cub Springs the other day to see if it were still flowing. We've been in a prolonged drought in Florida, an event that aids in the progressive destruction of natural landscapes around us. It is exacerbated by the great thirst of Floridians, a thirst that diminishes our already-stressed groundwater.

The springs are inside a state forest not far from my home. Although land around it is in public ownership, the delicate balance of its ecology is in jeopardy because the private land outside its boundaries affects its health. The vitality of our wild places in this sea-level state are often dependent on the kindness of strangers upstream—and the strangers have not always been kind. We have worked diligently over the last century to uproot our rare and wild places—dredging, draining, and burning it until little of its real spirit remains. Now, periodic droughts and the fires that follow in their wake continue that work. It was only logical I should worry about the health of a tiny spring.

Rock Cub is actually a series of four or five separate seeps that splay out of the bottom of a high bluff. The topographical map that first led me to it a few years ago showed the landscape dropping dramatically forty and fifty feet down a sloping terrain. At the bottom, the slope leveled out onto a blackwater swamp. The first time I walked down to the little springs, I had to hang onto the limbs of small water oaks and bay magnolias, grabbing the occasional frond of a sabal palm to keep from falling on my butt. There was no path here, not even one made by animals, and my only trail marker was the sense the bluff would, sooner or later, flatten out at the swamp below.

My most recent visit was more of the same—an ungraceful slow-mo freefall down the seepage slope, dodging the prickly cat briar vines and the finely woven web of the golden orb spiders. At the bottom, the springs still streamed from the base of the limestone bluff. The outflow was only a few inches deep but it was enough to polish the fine grains of silica and shell and limerock in the spring run so they glowed luminously when shafts of sunlight hit them. A limestone boulder in the shape of a bear cub sat in the middle, and the ether of the clear water flowed up and around it. I have visited this boulder and its springs during different seasons—by winter, with no foliage shade canopy, it is stark and bright, the rock itself clean and gray. By summer, with the thick crown of sweetgum and tupelo and oak above, and ferns, lichens, and mosses below, the scene changes: bromeliads spike the branches of the water oaks, and hidden in a crook, a spider orchid sends out a tentative, delicate bloom. Even the bear cub grows a rich coat of jade-colored mosses. The springs, insulated by the surrounding jungle, seem to actually resonate, refolding themselves into a gentle gurgle, as if the limerock bear itself has taken life and is sipping from them.

I wonder at the sheer timelessness of such places, of how swamps and seepage slopes that sometimes feed them are among the least changed of the Florida terrain. Too moist to burn, these relic landscapes have so far escaped the affliction that has reconfigured Florida, from the panhandle to the Keys. What I see today is similar to what other humans must have seen from the very moment this outlandish, wonderful peninsular geography took its present form.

These wetlands are our time machines, places that can transport us back to the geological beginnings, and if they afforded no other benefit, that alone would be worth the price of admission. But they allow a multitude of riches—storing and filtering water, keeping our climate and landscape moist, and housing a vast biological storehouse of animals and plants. It is no wonder that, over the last few centuries, naturalists like the Bartrams, Andre Michaux, A.W. Chapman, and John Kunkel Small—traveled to Florida as scientists journey to the deepest reaches of the Amazon or Africa today—to discover new species and to record new wonders.

It is in the re-reading of the vintage reports of their travels that we learn of early alarms that are now ringing so loudly they are impossible to ignore. In our Faustian bargains with land developers—who fund most successful political campaigns here—we are giving up the things that humans have loved most about Florida. When we canalize water and bulldoze the topsoil and plants from the wetlands and hammocks, we not only allow the moistness there to leak away—but also the birdsong, the star-filled night, the solitude, the wild spirit of a rare place.

Although naturalists had been warning about the over-harvesting of wildlife in the 19th century, it took botanist John Kunkel Small in the early 20th to alert us to the more profound damage we were inflicting on the ecological system itself. Wildlife, given good habitat, can return—unless of course, we blast them entirely out of existence. But when the ecology is altered, the existence of all living things becomes less certain.

Small, from the prestigious New York Botanical Garden, was a highly skilled botanist respected both for his field work as well as for his ability to discover or "describe" new plants. Small begin exploring Florida in 1901, driving a series of old jalopies he called his "weed wagons," zigzagging back and forth over dusty roads and into dense woods over the next three decades. Small particularly sought out plants that flourished in the rarefied habitats of "hammocks," from the Timucua-Taino word for *hamuca.* Hammocks are distinguished by the clustering of trees as revealed in the slightly higher tree islands that often sit atop marshland—sometimes even on the humus of ancient limestone outcroppings. Other hammocks are mesic or hydric—seasonally wet or nearly always wet. The mix of tropic and temperate plants and trees there spiked the diversity. Ferns, vines, and epiphytes turned the feral Florida landscape into a jungle.

Inside these hammocks, Small discovered specimens previously unknown to science. They thrived because of moisture and humidity, conditions underpinned by a high water table and abundant rainfall. Small traipsed through the hammocks and the woods of Ocala, Cedar Key, the Withlacoochee, and Crystal River. He crossed the interior to the Halifax River and then followed the Indian River Lagoon south, past Hobe Sound and Palm Beach. He zigzagged across the peninsula, heading inland across the prairie of the headwater marsh of the "Saint Johns River." Near Sanford, he noted the land had been transformed into a "vast vegetable garden" of celery, peppers, cabbage, and lettuce. In accurate and specific detail, Small uses his discriminating scientist's eye to describe a Florida that is no longer here, adding an ironic twist to his own eventual predictions.

When exploring the Daytona-New Smyrna area, he preferred using the geographic term "Tomoka" to illustrate it, as he felt the "modern designations are meaningless and inappropriate." Here during a Spring drought that rendered vegetation "puny," Small nonetheless collected river iris, a pitcher plant, sensitive briar, dwarf paw paw, and two species of orchid, among other plants. He also wisely noted the location of several Indian middens, observing that even when the shell was excavated for road fill, the site could be identified because the soil under them was rich, and thus supported a slightly different plant community.

During one of his trips, he found Bartram's Ixia, the striking wildflower that William Bartram had first described after spending a night camping on the east shore of Lake Dexter on the St. Johns in the late 1700's. The "cerulean Ixia" had never been seen in Florida after that, and had remained one of the great mysteries of Bartram's *Travels.* By 1931, Small rediscovered the Ixia, which now is scientifically known as *Calydorea coelestina.*

When Small roamed through Florida, the natural legacy of the place—lush, wet, soggy—was widely regarded as endless. "Improving" swamps by turning them into dry land was so accepted it became institutionalized in regional "Flood Control Districts." It was the way of progress, of civilizing this great peninsular wetland. But Small, a determined, impassioned man attenuated to the tiny nuances of a wildflower stamen and the cleft of its leaves, clearly saw an apocalyptic future. "The wholesale devastation of the plant covering, through carelessness, thoughtlessness, and vandalism in the Peninsula State...was everywhere apparent," Small observed.

Rare plant collectors would steal as many endemic orchids as they could find, and then burn the hammock they came from to make their specimens more valuable. State officials, happy with the newly-created dry patch of land, didn't seem to care. Yet individual collecting, as damaging as it was, was no match for the large state-funded drainage projects that cut canals to siphon away water, or which converted swamp to "productive" farmland.

In fact, extensive land development in Florida had begun after the Civil War. Early schemes to provide "waterfront property" in the form of canals along the coast served two purposes: It helped drain the wet landscape, and it created dry real estate that could be sold more expensively than interior land. As the coast became settled, developers moved inland to drain the swamps and marshes. The lords of canal building were Hamilton Disston, a wealthy Philadelphia manufacturer, and Henry Flagler, the railroad-building tycoon. The state of Florida offered free land to railroad building companies in exchange for opening up the interior frontier of Florida to train travel and transport. By 1881, the state had sold four million acres to Disston at the rate of 25 cents an acre on his promise to "drain" the entire Everglades from its origins just south of Orlando to Florida Bay. Disston's crews dynamited the waterfall on the Caloosahatchee River, dredged canals connecting Lakes Kissimmee, Tohopekeliga, and others in the headwaters. Before he died in 1904, he built hundreds of miles of canals and had drained nearly half a million acres.

In the early 1900's, Napoleon Bonaparte Broward successfully ran for governor on the promise to finish Disston's work. With a public tax-supported plan, he created the Everglades Drainage District. A 200-foot-wide canal drained Lake Okeechobee into the St. Lucie River, while the New River canal linked the larger inland lake with Ft. Lauderdale. Other rivers were straightened and deepened, including the Oklawaha and the Peace. A number of smaller lakes in Central Florida were connected by canals and locks.

Most thought wetlands to be troubling, and drainage to be a panacea that would allow the soggy, buggy peninsula to be settled. But while prosperity was promised, Small saw a more distressing impact the "reclamation" was having on the landscape.

By 1929, droughts, floods, and the deadly hurricanes of 1926 and 1928 had convinced legislators to form the Okeechobee Flood Control District and to issue additional bonds to generate funding for the completion of drainage projects, as well as to upshore and enlarge the dike around Okeechobee. Florida's population boom in the 1920's not only needed newly drained land, though, it needed potable water. Wells along the coast, where 80 percent of newcomers were settling, drew so heavily from the aquifer that salt soon intruded. Groundwater that nurtured swamps, marshes, and hammocks trickled away. Finally, the woods themselves were clear cut. Small's beloved orchids and wildflowers—including many specimens yet to be properly described—vanished. Small vividly witnessed the loss when he returned over the course of 30 years, and saw hammocks that were once vibrant and green, lush and mysterious, cut to the bare ground. It was heartbreaking, and he was both saddened and outraged by it.

By 1929, Small wrote this seminal book. In it, he predicted that if such drainage continued, Florida would become an arid wasteland. After all, it was on the same latitudes with the other great deserts of the world such as the Sahara. What kept Florida green was our groundwater and our wetlands. Small, who could be pigheadedly forthright, saw a "reckless, furious, even a mad desire to destroy everything natural." "The pecuniary greed of the native born and the immigrant is so great that few appear to be able or willing to see the handwriting on the map," wrote Small. "Not only are Fauna and Flora threatened with extermination, but in many places the very soil which is necessary to their production and maintenance is being drained and burned and re-burned until nothing but inert mineral matter is left." Small's book was instrumental in alerting the public to how the loss of wetlands and hammocks was more than a mere detail in the new growth and prosperity of Florida. Indeed, his concerns helped influence the movement to protect the Everglades in a national park, a deed finally accomplished in 1947.

Up until now, Small's classic book has been out of print. But like other earlier naturalists who visited the jungle that was once Florida, his caring for natural places and his concern for their conservation still rings true. "We try hard to preserve the old furniture that our ancestors sat and slept in," Small wrote, "but neglect the things that can never be replaced or even imitated."

I'll keep going back to my own relic of a historic Florida landscape, down the wooded slope to the hidden springs, because it is a place that can never be replaced or even imitated. Maybe if I don't neglect it, it might reward me by continuing to flow and to enchant.

But like everything else in modern Florida, the ecological indemnity of any place can no longer be assumed, whether it is publicly protected or not. Its health will require more than a large dose of faith. Indeed, it will take a deep-hearted love of nature and a pigheaded determination to not allow others to profit from its loss. It is a sentiment that botanist Small, a hardy explorer who cherished the enchantment of wildflowers, would have certainly appreciated.

Bill Belleville
2004

Introduction

Because of the magnitude and extent of changes to Florida's natural systems, ecologists are thirsty for reference points that shed light on historical conditions, patterns, and processes. Attempts to interpolate historical conditions from existing natural communities and/or records provide some reference for management, but are not always suitable to separate temporary changes in the landscape from the permanent effects of man's activities. Likewise, establishing goals for restoration is complicated by human influences and/or by a lack of knowledge about the historical characteristics of the natural system being restored. The siren call of documented historical conditions, especially from reputable sources, haunts restoration ecologists in their quest for understanding Florida's complex ecology. Thankfully, this call is occasionally answered through the exposure and distribution of significant, underrepresented works, such as the following work by John Kunkel Small. Based on his peregrinations in the 1920's, this lesser known work provides a significant reference point for the historical understanding of Florida ecology from the perspective of a renowned botanist and observant ecologist.

One interesting historical reference point recorded by Small is a record of the locations of shell middens and his treasured tropical hammocks. For instance, his careful notations about the specific locations of various shell middens were specifically logged to record "...their one-time location [that] can be determined in the future, when the shells will have been converted into highways...", or otherwise destroyed by other processes such as development. The point locations of these hammocks and middens provide not only sites of historical or cultural significance, but also a botanical and ecological legacy for the education of Floridians and scientists everywhere. His prescient notations about the fate of these communities, a process progressed even during his travels (to Green Mound), underlies one of his common themes of the loss of natural features. No doubt these communities were always unique, rare, and susceptible to relatively harsh forces of nature (hurricane, flood, fire). Still, these systems evolved in these areas, and could handle everything that nature could throw at them, except the advent of man's landscape-changing activities.

Small's copious notes about vegetation found on the mounds and the hammocks include many ecological gems, often consisting of notes about the distribution and relative abundance of species already considered imperiled or rare in his time and about species that have become imperiled in more recent years. In fact, of the plants identified in these unique ecosystems, two (*Talisia pedicellaris* and *Brassia caudata*) have not been seen in Florida in many years. Three of the plant species, including *Eriogonum floridanum, Harrisia fragrans,* and *Rhododendron chapmanii,* and one animal species (the Key deer, *Odocoileus virginianus clavium*) noted by Small are listed as threatened or endangered by the Federal government. All in all, at least 54 species of the plants noted by Small (approximately 12% of the total) in these unique habitats and throughout this manuscript are listed as threatened, endangered, or species of special concern by the state of Florida or the Federal government. In addition to adding important context to the historical understanding of imperiled species, Small's notes provide data ripe for further explorations to confirm and/or relocate populations of the rare species he mentions.

One of the other fascinating aspects of Small's manuscript is the documentation of the length of time that humans have been a force of change in the Florida landscape. Small refers to three epics in the natural history of Florida and poses the question about what changes will be realized during the fourth epic. Though, at times, Small laments the changes that have been exacted on Florida's natural systems by its native peoples, we could only imagine that Small would conclude that these changes were inconsequential in light of what actually has occurred in this "fourth epic" since Small's travels in Florida. In fact, current thought often includes Native Americans in Florida as generally a part of or significant force within the natural ecosystems. Yes, they changed the dynamics of some areas so that vegetative structure and function of those local ecosystems were dramatically affected from fire and flood, but their involvement seemed much more participatory in the natural processes and smaller in scale than modern man. The permanence of the effects of modern man's actions as forecasted by Small has been mostly realized in the last 80 years. The context of Florida ecology in Small's manuscript includes a detailed depiction of vegetative communities in the early 1920's drawn from his travels in the state that began right after the turn of the century. His manuscript also documents discussions with many Native Americans (including one who claimed to be over 100 years old) that provide at least a small window on the condition of the ecosystem during the reign of Native Americans.

The participatory nature of Native Americans is commonly referred to in Small's manuscript. Although he chastises the use of fire for anthropomorphic purposes, he comments favorably on the cultural and ecological significance of "farming" by the semi-nomadic native population. Coontie, cat-brier, red mulberry, lime, giant rooted morning-glory and the groundnut were undoubtedly utilized as food sources or trade items and transferred across the state to provide a perpetual stock of flour, fruit, building materials, etc. We are left with the intriguing task of assessing whether some of these populations are simply disjunct clusters of plant communities, or whether these distributions were driven by some long since forgotten use for some portion of the plant's roots, bark, fruit, leaves, or trunk. Additionally, his notes on Native American use of vegetation supply an interesting foundation for additional ethno-botanical explorations for modern day uses of these species.

Small provides an excellent source on the distribution of exotic species in the state. In some instances, exotic species generally thought to be relatively recently introduced into the state were common during the time of Small's trek across Florida. Species identified by Small as being exotic, including *Coreopsis lanceolata* and *Gaillardia drummondii,* are now considered to be native by modern texts (such as the *Guide to the Vascular Plants of Florida* by Wunderlin and Hansen, published in 2003). All told, Small noted at least 39 species of plants that are considered non-native and/or invasive in nature by modern sources. Small's observations on the status and relative distributions of exotic species and/or potentially exotic species can contribute significantly to the identification and dispersal history of exotic species that resource agencies now work so hard to remove.

Small's perspective on fire should also be a data point in our assessment of how to appropriately manage land and mimic historical patterns of fire. Likely, his musings reflected the fire suppression mindset that was pervasive in his time and continued until a few decades ago. This mindset resulted in modified conditions throughout Florida, currently understood to be detrimental to rare and common species within pyrophilic plant communities, such as sandhills and flatwoods. The shift from suppression to a prescribed application of fire within the last twenty to thirty years is, we hope, based on a thorough understanding of the importance of fire in the Florida (and Coastal Plain) landscape. Although systems now thought to depend on frequent fires benefit from this focus on fire reintroduction, Small's concerns for less fire-dependent communities such as shell middens, hammocks, and even scrub should continue to remind us to proceed with caution when instituting resource management efforts that could result in significant changes in vegetative composition and structure.

Still, we have no doubt that Small recognized these factors, and based some of his conclusions about the devastating effects of fire with full knowledge of the implications of fire-tolerant and pyrogenic species of plants. His review and conclusions may, however, have been affected by the time of year (at the end of the rainy season), an extended drought that may have occurred at the end of his travels, and the widespread drainage he describes. We should be careful to consider Small's input on the effects of fire, along with the conclusions about vegetative communities that might have occurred prior to and after the occurrence of fires noted by Small. These data points will serve us well in defining fire return intervals in areas where fire is now thought to be an important aspect of community ecology.

Likewise, Small's observations on hydrology are of great benefit in studying the hydrology of many vegetative communities in Florida. Small's treatise provides documentation of the fervor with which we actively "improved" swamplands that were otherwise inhospitable to man. The extent of man's historical (and recent) actions within the state changed the frequency, duration, and extent of flooding within thousands of acres of wetlands. Our recent focus on the restoration of many of these wetlands has been significantly compromised by the extent of major surface and groundwater drainage alterations, many of which were begun before the 1920's. Still, restoration efforts ranging from comprehensive ecosystem-level major projects (Comprehensive Everglades Restoration Program, and Kissimmee River Restoration projects) to projects with more of a regional or local focus are ongoing in south and central Florida. Perhaps some of the deleterious effects of surface and groundwater alterations may be successfully ameliorated with enough time and effort (money). Small's manuscript provides an historical context with which to frame some if these efforts.

There is some good news since the time of Small's writings. He admonished public officials, and in some respects the public itself, to act swiftly to protect Florida's natural systems while there was still time. In the last few decades, agencies at local, state, and federal levels have purchased millions of acres of natural lands in Florida, restored natural patterns of fire and hydrology in many of these areas, and nullified some of the effects of historical changes in the landscape. Water management districts now enforce regulations aimed to protect and restore surface and groundwater hydrology, and a regulatory framework is in place to protect listed species of plants and animals. Development pressures abound, and changes in Florida's landscape are still occurring at a remarkable rate. However, in part because of the writings and attention drawn by manuscripts such as the one prepared by Small, we understand the ramifications of these changes, and have sought ways to ameliorate the impacts proposed by human-induced changes. Yes, there still is time to protect a broad expanse of Florida natural systems, and we should heed the cautionary words of Small, and seek to protect these natural systems with continued vigilance.

Jay Exum, Ph.D. and Randy Mejeur, M.S.
2004

Original Preface

The following pages contain a continuous narrative of botanical exploration of several thousand miles in the Florida peninsula and on the Florida Reef or Continental Shelf, from the middle of April to the middle of May, 1922. The observations, facts, and fancies are recorded in chronological order.

The wholesale devastation of the plant covering, through carelessness, thoughtlessness, and vandalism in the Peninsular State, prehistoric and historic, was everywhere apparent. Frequent references to it are made in the narrative and special examples are mentioned in detail. A series of pictures is inserted through the text with which they are directly or indirectly connected. They show, in each case, localities as adorned by nature and as "improved" by man. It may be said, however, that the plant covering has had to contend with destruction and changes for ages, and would reassert itself in one form or another in time. For example, local hammocks and pinelands might restore themselves in comparatively short periods, but the Lake Okeechobee region might take a million years

On the other hand, the Florida aborigines are extinct and the ruins of their civilization will soon be gone, too. These peoples will never reassert themselves. The remains of their blood is in some of the inhabitants of Cuba and of southern Mexico, to which countries the Spanish invaders removed a few of them as slaves.

We have good evidence that man occupied Florida as early as the Pleistocene age. How many distinct prehistoric occupations may have occurred we do not know; nor do we know whence came the prehistoric-historic aborigines referred to in the following narrative. The ranks of these peoples were greatly reduced four centuries ago. About two centuries later the remnants disappeared from the Florida peninsula.

The destruction of aboriginal village sites, kitchen-middens, burial mounds, and ceremonial structures is progressing without any attempt at a scientific study and interpretation, not to mention preservation. Many such structures have been demolished merely for the sake of getting trinkets and curiosities.

The present population of Florida is wholly of recent alien stock or immigrant. The Seminole Indians—Creeks from Georgia and Alabama—moved into the peninsula following the disappearance of the Apalachee from northern Florida and other aborigines from the peninsula, and the rest of the population has been gathered together from every corner of the earth, mainly within the past fifty years.

To recapitulate: A country unique in its geologic structure, its geographic position, and its plant covering, is not merely interesting, but a close study of it is extremely fascinating. Its surface has had three epochs with which we are more directly concerned, that is, the period since man appeared on the scene. The first is mostly prehistoric, extending from the Pleistocene age down to about two centuries ago, when the aboriginal human inhabitants were exterminated. Through this epoch nature constructed and man was comparatively inactive. The second epoch may be termed neutral, for the peninsula for about a century had a rest from man's activities and nature was largely in a condition of *status quo.*

The third epoch is eminently historic. Its record shows a reckless, furious, even a mad desire to destroy everything natural. This epoch began about a century ago when the red man and the white man pushed into the peninsula and contended through several bloody wars for the occupancy of the land. The red man was submerged. The white man has become increasingly active in transforming the surface of the peninsula. The question is, what will be the fourth epoch?

J.K.S
301 East 207th Street,
New York City, N.Y.
1929

From Eden to Sahara: Florida's Tragedy

The past of the Peninsular State is partly revealed both by its geology and by the monuments left there by the aborigines. The present is evident. The future may confidently be predicted, in part, by the aims and the actions of the white man—he who began, and has consistently persevered in, a course of devastation almost unequaled elsewhere. Beginning in the earliest post-Columbian times, this reckless, even wanton, devastation has now gained such headway that the future of North America's most prolific paradise seems to spell DESERT. The pecuniary greed of the native born and the immigrant is so great that few appear to be able or willing to see the handwriting on the—map (with apologies to the Prophet Daniel). Not only are Fauna and Flora threatened with extermination, but in many places the very soil which is necessary to their production and maintenance is being drained and burned and reburned until nothing but inert mineral matter is left.

In some ways man has progressed in ideas and in methods within the past few centuries. In other ways he is still typically a "savage." Certain methods of life of the savage–uncivilized red man and the savage-civilized white man are identical. The following quotation written four centuries ago about the aboriginal red man applies just as well to his pale-faced successor of today: "Those from further inland have another remedy, just as bad and even worse, which is to go about with a firebrand, setting fire to the plains and timber so as to drive off the mosquitoes, and also to get lizards and similar things which they eat to come out of the soil. In the same manner they kill deer, encircling them with fires, and they do it also to deprive the animals of pasture, compelling them to go for food where the Indians want. For never they build their abodes except where there are wood and water, and sometimes load themselves with the requisites and go in quest of deer, which are found mostly where there is neither water nor wood."[1]

We started south from New York after a prolonged, though not a severe winter. The landscape generally was not strikingly green as a whole. Many native trees, however, had begun to unfold their leaf-buds, and such cultivated trees and shrubs as the peach, pear, apple, magnolia, yellow-bells, and maples had opened their flower buds.

The natural plant covering was brown or gray-brown, except in the swamps and marshes, which were often rendered green by the numerous tufts of sedges *(Carex)* and rushes *(Juncus).* Flowering herbs were scarce; those more conspicuously occupying the high and low lands, respectively, were the dandelion *(Leontodon)* and the skunk-cabbage *(Spathyema).*

The habits and habitats of the individual pin-oak *(Quercus rubra)* in the north reminded us of the still greater live-oak *(Q. virginiana)* in the south. The variation of the leaves and the branching and its adaptation to both wet and dry situations are common to both.

The contrast of the precocity and the tardiness of the leafing of trees was interesting; the former was represented by the birches and the maples, the latter by some of the oaks and the honey-locusts. In some places the wild or semi-wild cherry trees showed an abundance of blossoms suggestive of the elegant cultivated Japanese cherries. Toward southern Pennsylvania the landscape became gradually greener. However, the more striking trees were the dead ones, skeletons of conifers, mostly the Norway-spruce *(Picea abies)* which was so much in vogue on country estates several generations ago.

The most unusual sight, however, was an old-fashioned canal-boat drawn indirectly by the energy furnished by living vegetation (mule-power) in great contrast to the usual methods of modern motive power whose energy is furnished by fossil plants (coal).

The budding trees emphasized the various kinds of branching and the consequent shapes. For example, the maples were *bush-like,* the elms *plume-like,* the hickories *cylindric,* the walnuts *globular,* and the red-cedars *conic.*

In Delaware and Maryland the dogwood *(Cynoxylon)* and the wild-plum *(Prunus)* were in flower, and about the latitude of Baltimore and Washington, the leaves were grown enough to make a half screen, and lilacs were in bloom about houses. Although few shrubs were in flower the arrangement of the unfolding leaves often simulated flowers, especially when viewed from a distance.

Colonies of half-grown may-apple *(Podophyllum)* plants appeared on the hillsides conspicuous on account of the parasol-like leaves. However, the pinewoods still had their nearly uniform brown carpet. Finally a flowering shrub appeared, the lambkill *(Neopieris mariana)* with its tiered clusters of pinkish-white nodding flowers on wand-like stems. A more unusual shrub, witch-alder *(Fothergilla),* moreover, grew here and there in small colonies. It has subterranean stems and clustered greenish-yellow flowers, prominent on account of the numerous relatively long stamens. Its leaves resemble those of the witch-hazel *(Hamamelis)* to which plant it is really closely related. The decided color in the landscape, however, was furnished by the birds-foot violet *(Viola pedata),* large patches of which, with its bright-colored flowers, burst into view many times.

In the Carolinas the leaves of shrubs and trees nearly or quite full-grown, formed complete screens particularly brilliant on account of their still virgin green. Finally, the white festoons of the fringe-tree and other flowers were more in evidence. Bright-colored salvias decorated the high-land woods, while flags and pitcher plants colonized in the marshes and swamps. Blackberry bushes formed tangles in the thickets. Masses of roots from the nearby woody plants lined the streams in hammocks, and standing water was covered with water-lilies and bladderworts. The earliest bloomer of the swamps was in evidence by its almost gigantic leaves—the golden-club *(Orontium).* This plant, curiously enough, is common from the Ten Thousand Islands of southern Florida nearly up to the latitude of the Thousand Islands of Canada. Here and there violets *(Viola),* arrowheads *(Sagittaria),* rock-roses *(Crocanthemum),* ragworts *(Senecio),* and the very brilliant phlox *(Phlox amoena)* appeared.

Two plants were particularly attractive—the curious but striking false-indigo *(Baptisia alba)* with its tiered clusters of bright-white flowers and the swamp wisteria *(Bradleya frutescens),* which decorated the shrubs and trees of swamps in a gorgeous manner.

South of the Altamaha River, the hammock growth was changed in character. The loblolly-bay *(Gordonia lasianthus)* and the sweet-bay *(Magnolia virginiana),* both with white fragrant flowers, were often the most prominent trees.

Our course in the southern states lay wholly in the Coastal Plain. This is an interesting region from many standpoints. Geologically, it is the youngest and newest part of North America. It abuts on the oldest part of the continent—the Piedmont Plateau. Much of the Coastal Plain is still in the making, or is it unmaking? Is the land rising or sinking? Vast areas, at any rate, can scarcely be called wet or dry. They are both. The average water-table is just about the level of the surface of the soil, hence such vast regions are both uninhabited and uncultivated. From the Piedmont, the Coastal Plain received the greater part of its flora, the ancestors of the plants now to be found there. Of course, other elements have come in from the north and from the West Indies, through the agency of migratory birds, winds, and ocean currents. All except two of our southeastern States comprise several geologic ages. South of the Saint Mary's River, or in Florida, there is only one formation represented—the Coastal Plain. The following matter is concerned with Florida, but in passing it may be of interest to note that

Mississippi also lies wholly within the Coastal Plain.

One of the major objects of our excursion was the exploration of the surface of aboriginal Indian village sites, kitchen-middens, and burial grounds and their relative positions.

Kitchen-Middens of the Upper Eastern Coast

We passed by the mounds at the mouth of the Saint John's River for the present and proceeded from Jacksonville to the scene of the greatest aboriginal "shell-fish industry" in Florida, the Daytona-New Smyrna region, or as the aborigines would have had it, the Tomoka region—a better term, for the two modern geographic designations are both meaningless and inappropriate.

A seven months' drought had rendered floriferous vegetation backward or puny, especially in the earlier part of our course. A few herbs and shrubs were flowering along the way. Among them were blue-flags *(Iris),* a pitcher-plant *(Sarracenia),* sensitive-brier *(Leptoglottis),* yellow bachelor's-button *(Polygala),* St. Peter's-wort *(Ascyrum),* sage *(Salvia),* dwarf-pawpaw *(Asimina),* a sand-blackberry *(Rubus),* gopher-apple *(Geobalanus),* prickly-pear *(Opuntia),* fetter-bush *(Leucothoë)*—mostly plants of the lower situations.

The hammocks[2] showed brilliant greens on account of the fresh foliage, and although no showy flowers were open, the leaves of the sweet-bay *(Magnolia)* upturned by the breezes appeared as numerous large white flowers in the distance.

Wet meadows appeared floriferous by the new mottled leaves of the small pitcher-plant *(Sarracenia minor).* Two terrestrial orchids were not uncommon, the one white and rather inconspicuous *(Ibidium laciniatum),* the other colored and showy, the grass-pink *(Limodorum).* In one low place the resemblance between the inflorescence of two unrelated plants was striking. The white spikes of the devil's-bit *(Chamaelirium),* a monocotyledon, and those of the lizard's-tail *(Saururus)* were quite similar in habit.

In the damp meadows patches of two members of the bunch-flower family were frequent. They were fly-poisons *(Chrosperma and Tracyanthus).* The dry lands were sometimes conspicuous on account of two composites—a hawkweed *(Hieracium)* and a false-aster *(Doellingeria).* In damp pinewoods[3] there was often a patch of the atamas-lily *(Atamosco),* while in the palmetto-land plants of *Tracyanthus* commonly raised their white plumes above the saw-palmetto leaves, on slender or nearly invisible stalks.

We soon reached the land of monumental aboriginal activities—the coastal dunes and the adjacent mainland of the Halifax River region. The woody vegetation of the dunes is very extensive and diverse. In addition to the native herbs, some of which, such as the scarlet-sage and spiderwort, are plentiful and showy, several exotics have become widely naturalized and thoroughly at home. Prominent among these are: phlox *(Phlox drummondii),* blanket-weed *(Gaillardia drummondii),* tickseed *(Coreopsis lanceolata),* and golden crownbeard *(Ximenesia encelioides).*

The lagoon, in this case the so-called Halifax River, was the main reason for the aboriginal activities, for there was an inexhaustible supply of oysters in its waters. The ocean, too, furnished a greater variety of "shell-fish," but in lesser abundance. The dunes from Ocean City down to the toll chain of the inland water-way show scarcely any remains of aboriginal occupation. The absence of aboriginal activities is indicated by the absence of hammocks on these sands. Viewed from an elevated point the vegetation of these dunes gives the impression of a vast undulating evenly mowed lawn of as many shades of green as there are different kinds of shrubs. The shrubs are low and intricately branched with the branchlets often woven into a coarse fabric. The whole growth might be considered a pygmy hammock. The stunted growth is doubtless caused by both the lack of food and lack of moisture in the sand. The intricate branching may result in the shielding and protection of their roots from the sun. The pruning is done by the continuous sweeping winds and wind-blown sand, for it is most thoroughly done on the windward side.

Closely examined, the elements of the dune vegetation are scrub-oak *(Quercus),* red- bays *(Tamala),* cassena *(Ilex),* wax-myrtle *(Cerothamnus),* toothache-tree *(Zanthoxylum),* and saw-palmetto *(Serenoa),* and toward the lagoon or away from the ocean some cabbage-trees *(Sabal)* frequently rise above the general plant cover. The green and white clumps of saw-palmetto often arise from the vast beds of brilliant green scrub-oaks. Herbs are scarce at all times. The ones of prominence were the dune-verbena *(Verbena maritima)* and the scarlet-sage *(Salvia coccinea).* But to come to the kitchen-middens. These will be mentioned here in some detail because they are fast disappearing, as are all the natural and aboriginal monuments of Florida, through one of the universally evident negative characteristics of the white man. Our interest in these monuments has been increased of late, and their exact position has been located through the activities in the field and the exact observations of Ethel Anson S. Peckham during the winter of 1922. By recording the exact position of each shell midden in that region, their one-time location can be determined in the future, when the shells will have been converted into highways which in turn will some day be constructed of material foreign to that region or even to the State.

A large midden borders the north side of Tomoko Creek at the head of the Halifax River. Starting southward at the Iron Bridge over the inland waterway, we find at 0.6 of a mile an oval midden. Extending from 1.3–1.4 miles is a larger midden composed mostly of oyster-shells and clam-shells. At 1.5–1.7 miles the midden comprises besides shells of the oyster, the clam, and the conch, those of several smaller kinds of bivalves. At 2.1 miles the midden is mostly dug away, and that at 2.3 miles is in the same condition. At 2.7 miles the midden consists of oyster-shells and conch-shells, together with those of several less common kinds of shells, and between 3.3 and 3.4 miles a midden comprising the same kind of shells exists. Between 4.5 and 4.7 miles the midden, in addition to oyster-shells and clam-shells, showed those of the conch and donax. At 5.7 miles there is a small midden. At 6.3 is another midden from which the shells have been removed. Between 6.5 and 6.7 miles a midden rich in hammock growth is conspicuous. Its arboreous covering comprises large trees of hickory *(Hicoria),* red-bay *(Tamala),* live-oak *(Quercus),* red-cedar *(Sabina),* slash-pine *(Pinus),* and cabbage-trees *(Sabal).* At about 9.6 miles there is a burial mound made up of humus and shells mixed with sand. The bones of the skeletons are much decayed principally as a result of the acids from the humus. Pieces of pottery were not rare in the mound which is built up on a shell midden and now supports large trees of slash-pine and saw-palmetto. There were masses or clusters of small shells in the mound, perhaps placed there to be used by the spirits of the dead on their way to the happy hunting grounds.

In passing it may be of interest to note that although these shell mounds may be destroyed to the extent of the removal of most of the shells and the consequent obliteration of elevation, their location will be evident for generations to come by the native vegetation of each site. The soil under kitchen-middens is usually very rich and supports a vegetation differing from that thereabouts.

The presence of a kitchen-midden is indicated by the plant growth. These dunes are naturally covered with a scrubby growth of shrubs and small trees, but wherever there is a shell-midden, we find a dense hammock, usually so dense that herbaceous and shrubby growth is sparse. The most interesting phenomena connected with the vegetation are the tropical elements there represented. The wild-coffee *(Psychotria undata)* and the snowberry *(Chiococca alba)* are there. The interest is not confined to terrestrial plants, however, for in these midden hammocks the range of tropical tree-orchid *(Encyclia tampensis)* overlaps that of the temperate tree-orchid *(Amphiglottis conopsia).*

The southern part of the Halifax River is, and was, more productive of oysters than the northern, hence the more striking monumental aboriginal mounds. Their location on the coastal dunes is as follows: starting at the eastern end of the "stone bridge" at Daytona Beach and going toward the Mosquito Inlet light-house, we find what has been termed the Two House Mound[4] at 4.2 miles south. It is composed mostly of oyster-shells and clam-shells. The shell-middens south of Daytona Beach are higher than those to the north. The water-table is, naturally, far below the surface and the vegetation is much more stunted, yet it is prolific, and its tropical character is evident. The woody growth is mainly wild-coffee *(Psychotria undata),* snowberry *(Chiococca alba),* stopper *(Eugenia axillaris),* marlberry *(Icacorea paniculata),* and spice-tree *(Anamomis simpsonii).* At 5.4 miles are the remains of an immense midden composed of oyster-shells and clam-shells, with a mixture also of conch-shells and those of several smaller kinds. Much shell material has been removed for building roads. The remains are about thirty feet high, and concreted mass of shells indicating the spot where continual fires were maintained, surmounts it. This fireplace is cubic, and like a castle perched on top of a hill. Hence the name Castle Mound has been applied to this midden. It measures about eight by ten feet and the top stands about six feet above the top of the loose shells. It was formerly larger, but it is gradually wearing away, and at no distant day the county road-makers will demolish it.[5] Vegetation has invaded this crown—eight kinds in all: spice-tree *(Anamomis simpsonii),* bayberry *(Cerothamnus ceriferus),* sisal *(Agave rigida),* gum-elastic *(Bumelia tenax),* shrubby-verbena *(Lantana ovaltifolia),* and the papaya *(Carica papaya).* It was of interest to observe the peculiar shade of green of the spice-tree on these middens as compared with its associates. Several shrubs and trees of the myrtle family have a striking, a very unusual shade of green in their leaves. It sets them off from all their associates, even from members of their own family. The myrtle-of-the-river *(Calyptranthes zuzygium)* of the hammocks of the Everglade Keys in southern peninsular Florida has the same characteristic.

Small middens occur at 6.2 miles and 6.5 miles. At 7 miles there is a large mound. At 8 miles there is a very large midden, locally called "Green-Mound," and at 10 miles lies another. An excavation at Green-Mound gave a perpendicular section of about twelve feet. The contents were mostly oyster-shells, clam-shells, and conch-shells with large layers or clusters of small shells placed here and there. There is little extraneous matter in the midden—only some layers of humus and charcoal, indicating successive occupations, and bones of animal and rarely a human skeleton. Especially interesting were the large epiphysial plates from the spinal-column of a whale which was evidently stranded on the beach near there centuries ago and doubtless feasted on by the aborigines. These bony structures resemble gigantic lima-beans and when removed from the surrounding shells, promptly crumbled.

Continuing our journey southward we crossed the lagoon to the mainland to investigate another series of middens. There is little or nothing in the way of shell mounds between Daytona and Port Orange on the mainland, although judging from the character of the vegetation the region was a favorite one for village sites. But, starting southward at the end of the Port Orange bridge, we find a midden at 1.2 miles. At 2 miles there is a midden on a sand bar near the shore. Beginning at 2.2 miles there is an immense midden a great deal of which has been removed for road-building material. Smaller mounds occur at 3.5 miles, 3.6 miles, and 4.2 miles. Another very large one is located at 4.7 miles. At 5.5 miles shell heaps reappear, and a large one is located at 6.7 miles. The last one of this series is located at 7 miles.

These middens maintain a growth of shrubs and trees similar to that on the coastal dunes, and also other kinds representing more temperate types. Some of them have a remarkable covering of the wild-pepper plant *(Peperomia cumulicola)* and the little spiderwort *(Tradescantella floridana),* both of which thrive best in a soil in which humus predominates over mineral matter. Curiously enough, this wild-pepper plant has not been found except on aboriginal ruins; the spiderwort is more often seen on such habitats than elsewhere.

Having crossed the marshes inside of Mosquito Inlet and reached New Smyrna, we crossed over to the coastal dunes at Coronado. At 2.6 miles south of Coronado there are some large mounds composed of oyster-shells, clam-shells, conch-shells, and those of donax. One of these mounds represents the northern geographic limit of the prickly-apple *(Harrisia fragrans)* first found on the dunes south of Fort Pierce, but since collected at several points along the lower eastern coast where it is endemic. This is a "night-blooming cereus" of which there are many kinds in the tropics. There are three kinds of *Harrisia* in Florida; besides the one above mentioned, one on the western coast of the peninsula and one in the Cape Sable region and on the Florida Keys. In spring the plants bear an abundance of large white trumpet-shaped flowers that open almost uniformly at ten o'clock in the evening; these are followed by round red or yellow apple-like fruits, whence the popular name. The plants thrive in cultivation.

Two of the commoner trees appeared of especial interest in regard to their bark, particularly the reason for the differences as they grow under the same conditions. In other words, why should the live-oak have such a thick and rugged bark, while its associate the spice-tree has a thin, conspicuously smooth bark? The question has not been answered. The conspicuous herbaceous plant in bloom was the maypop *(Passiflora incarnata).* This is one of the few plants that range all the way from the southern low country up into the mountains! Its common name refers to the explosive sound given off by the fruits when stepped on in May when they are nearly or quite ripe.

Having finished our studies on the kitchen-middens of the Halifax River region, we set out for the opposite side of the peninsula. From Daytona to the Saint John's River, after leaving the coastal hammocks, we crossed a succession of pineland, scrub,[6] low hammocks, cypress swamps, and prairies. Greenery was plentiful in spite of the drought, for the country is low, but flowers were rare, except where yellow woody sand-weed *(Hypericum fasciculatum)* and ragwort *(Senecio lobatus)* were massed; while the saw-palmetto *(Serenoa repens)* and the gallberry *(Ilex galbra),* often everbloomers and lemon-drops *(Sitilias caroliniana),* so called from their lemon-yellow flower heads, lined the roadsides. On the hills east of the Saint John's River two deeply rooted perennials with subterranean food reservoirs bloomed profusely. They were the green-eye *(Berlandiera humilis)* and pine-pink *(Lygodesmia aphylla).* On descending to the swamps of the Saint John's two plants were more striking than their associates—the one woody, cypress *(Taxodium distichum),* the other herbaceous, the South American water-milfoil *(Myriophyllum proserpinacoides),* which carpeted the cypress swamps with a brilliant green and which was associated here and there with darker green patches of the aromatic basil *(Clinopodium glabrum).*

Crossing from a more or less untamed country on the eastern side of the river, we entered a highly cultivated land in the vicinity of Sanford. The western old flood plain of the Saint John's has been transformed into a vast vegetable garden where "weeds" vie with "truck" for the supremacy. The ragweed *(Ambrosia artemisiifolia)* was as high as one's head, and fields of celery, peppers, cabbage, lettuce, and other vegetables often stretched in the distance as far as the eye could see.

Continuing westward black-jack ridges appeared as we

reached the heart of the lake region.[7] The black-jack or turkey-oak *(Quercus catesbaei)* had put on its very bright-green new leaves which in the fall were to become, as described in a former article,[8] a brilliant red. In crossing these ridges we were struck with the character of the bark of the oaks and the pines. The oaks *(Quercus cinerea)* are very rough, deeply furrowed, and ridged. They, too, are like the pines with which they are associated, of striking gray color. Why? These questions also came to mind, why are pinelands? Why are black-jack ridges? Why is scrub?

On the hills in the lake region[9] a few kinds of plants had put forth flowers showing some variety in color—among them the delicate spiderwort *(Cuthbertia),* queen's-root *(Stillingia),* golden-saucers *(Piriquita),* tread-softly *(Cnidoscolus),* calophanes *(Dyschoriste),* umbrella-plant *(Eriogonum).* It is of interest to note that all these plants have drought-resisting roots or subterranean food-reservoirs. About the lakes there were vast stretches of the colorless fire-weed *(Erechtites)* or the highly colored pickerel-weed or wampee *(Pontederia).* The low hammocks were conspicuous with borders of white-flowered elder trees *(Sambucus)* or the yellow-flowered evening-primrose *(Jussiaea),* both of which bloom nearly or quite the year round. These plants are widely distributed, for their fruits are adapted to easy dispersal. Those of the former are fleshy and eaten by birds; those of the latter burst and scatter the dust-like seeds which are carried far by the winds. A favorite garden plant in the towns was the Florida century-plant *(Agave neglecta).* This elegant succulent was discovered in the Tomoka region nearly two centuries ago by the Bartrams, but it was without a correct botanical name until the beginning of this century.

From the lake region we passed into the lime-sink[10] region—now an agricultural district. Here a favorite flower-garden plant was the spineless cactus *(Opuntia ficus-indica),* which was often seen in full bloom.

Old farming country had two marks of identification: the one the avenues of old oaks planted by the pioneers along the roads many years ago; the other, the presence of "weeds"—Natal-grass *(Tricholaena)* of recent introduction, but now thoroughly naturalized, and the old-fashioned Jamestown-weed or Jimson-weed *(Datura stramonium).* Abandoned fields were prolific nurseries for the clotbur *(Xanthium)* making millions of seeds to scatter and infest other localities.

About sundown we crossed from the lime-sink region into the wild and more sparsely settled Gulf Hammock[11] region, and after dark continued our journey until we reached Crystal River.

Kitchen-Middens of the Upper Western Coast

Many evidences of aboriginal activity now confronted us, as they already had on the eastern coast—a region of shell-middens and consequently a more than ordinarily interesting flora. Crystal River, like the lagoons along the eastern coast, was an ideal place for both the oyster and the red man, and, in addition, the latter had the great Gulf Hammock to draw on for various other meats in addition to the fish and oyster of the waters. The settlement of Crystal River is situated at the head of the river of the same name, which arises abruptly as a spring and flows through a wet plain a dozen miles westward to the Gulf. In the morning we procured a mother-boat and started down the river. We stopped at Spanish Mound, which is situated less than half way down the stream. Its floristics were referred to in a former article.[12] Out of curiosity we measured the mound. It extends about sixty feet east and west, about one hundred and six feet north and south, and is thirty-two feet high. The evident shells which comprise it are oyster, the clam *(Venus),* and the conch. There are several smaller mounds near the large one and a village site adjoining it. The mound itself and its environs are clothed with hammock. More than a dozen kinds of trees were common: among them were the magnolia *(Magnolia foetida),* sweet-bay *(Magnolia virginiana),* swamp-bay *(Tamala pubescens),* linden *(Tilia heterophylla),* hickory *(Hicoria glabra),* live-oak *(Quercus virginiana),* choke-cherry *(Padus virginiana),* ash *(Fraxinus lanceolata),* soapberry *(Sapindus marginatus),* persimmon *(Diospyros virginiana),* water-oak *(Quercus nigra).* Vines and recliners were plentiful—such as the grape *(Vitis aestivalis),* spiny buckthorn *(Sageretia minutiflora),* and the snowberry *(Chiococca alba).* Of particular interest were the big trees of the hickory and sweet-bay, which were often over three feet in diameter. The mulberry *(Morus rubra)* was much in evidence, as it is also on and about nearly every aboriginal settlement. The Indians doubtless used the fruits as food, and it is a matter of record that they employed the inner bark for clothing, such as they used.

We landed, for a short time, at the large shell-midden at the mouth of the river. This structure and its plants have been described in detail in a former article.[13] The two more conspicuous plants at this season were the Spanish-bayonet *(Yucca aloifolia)* and cool-and-easy *(Zanthoxylum clava-herculis).* Both of these were formerly much used by the pioneer. The leaves of the Spanish-bayonet contain an exceedingly strong fiber which was used in cases where a strong string or rope was needed. The cool-and-easy or toothache-tree was used as a toothache remedy—giving to the mouth, as the name implies, a refreshing, astringent feeling. Citrus trees—lemon and orange—were there also, perhaps the descendants of plants introduced when the Spaniards were active in that region.

Large-"rooted" plants are a feature of this midden. Of course, the so-called "root" of the coontie *(Zamia)* is the stem of the plant. The largest underground structure of the midden, however, is a real root which produces numerous herbaceous vines *(Ipomoea).* The usual symmetry of these bulky underground structures is quite remarkable when we consider the great and uneven pressure required to make places for themselves in the firmly packed masses of shells. These great ipomoea roots, some large enough to fill a bushel basket, were sending out new tender branches, while some had the old stems attached which bore the remains of morning-glory pods from which we even secured a few seeds. Perhaps this root was one of the economic plants of the aborigines, for it is found only on or about the kitchen-middens. The largest root collected weighed fifty-two and a half pounds several months after it was out of the shell-heap. The most abundant shrub was the snowberry *(Chiococca),* which almost completely covered the shells with a thick green carpet of matted stems and leaves, over which were frequently scattered clusters of white flowers and ivory-like fruits. Toward the water, where visitors are accustomed to land, weeds had crept into the native plant association. We noticed the wild-carrot *(Daucus pusillus),* sow-thistle *(Sonchus oleraceus),* beggar's-ticks *(Bidens leucantha),* pepper-grass *(Lepidium virginicum),* and goose-foot *(Chenopodium album).*

The sight of the delta of the Withlacoochee six or seven miles up the coast from the mouth of the Crystal River was too enticing to resist, so we headed our boat northward for Port Inglis. Except for an army surgeon, Dr. G. W. Hulse, during the Seminole wars, botanists had not visited that locality. Dr. Hulse collected specimens of *Zamia* there and wrote about them, as recorded in a former article.[14] From this part the Florida phosphate rock was formerly shipped to Germany. The place is now almost deserted. We were greeted by a pack of some eighteen hungry dogs, however, who gave us a noisy, but, fortunately, not a touching welcome. We soon located the *Zamia* we sought. It grew luxuriantly in the shells of the kitchen-midden and in shell soil. Although *Zamia* represents a group which may be considered a remnant, as it were, of a former geologic era, its present representatives are not easy to exterminate, else the natural supply in Florida would be nearer the verge of extinction than it is today.[15]

This delta, inhabited by the aborigines for ages, has also

been settled by the white man for many years. Some of the old red-cedars *(Sabina silicicola)* looked as if they might have been there at the end of the red-man's occupation. The white man has left his mark by leveling off the top of shell-mounds for buildings and gardens, and by such exotic and now naturalized plants as sweet-alyssum *(Koniga maritima),* peach *(Amygdalus persica),* and fig *(Ficus carica).* The water hyacinth, too, was floating about in the labyrinth of channels.

A high tide enabled us to run back to the Crystal River rather close to the Gulf shore. The palmetto-clad shore and atoll-like islands continually invited an inspection of their sandy or wood-clad shore. Then, too, there are two small shell-middens on the shore in Boggy Bay and one built up on an island two miles off shore. Our intended trip up Salt River necessitated haste in that direction. A number of interesting shell-mounds exist in its upper reaches.[16] However, the day was so far spent that we could devote a short time to only one mound before Salt River was reached. There we found the skeleton of a large whale that had been blown ashore during a storm three or four years before. The skeleton was of particular interest to us because it solved the problem of the strange bones, the epiphysial plates mentioned on a preceding page, we found in the shell-midden south of Daytona. We found our way back into Crystal River, where the horizontal rays of the sun silhouetted the cabbage-trees *(Sabal palmetto),* with their pale trunks and bright green crowns against the more somber green of the deep hammocks. While going up the river, the air about sundown was laden with the fragrance of the big-magnolia *(Magnolia foetida),* the sweet-bay *(Magnolia virginiana),* and the grape *(Vitis),* blended in varying degrees.

The preceding pages refer much to Florida's yesterday through the kitchen-middens. Approaching the head of the river the view of the large pencil factory at Crystal River brought to mind the evolution of Florida's today and reminded us of the fast approaching extermination of native floral life in Florida. The red-cedar is being used up for lead-pencils—or should we say, has been; the pine for fruit-crates, the hickory for wheel-spokes and tool-handles. The animals, even in the deepest hammocks, are likewise being exterminated—for "sport"; and the ground itself is being drained and burned until it is unproductive. What is to be Florida's tomorrow?

Early the following morning we set out for the Pinellas Peninsula. We had to go inland to Inverness, crossing ridges of barren country until we got back into the agricultural belt. Turning southward at Inverness, we visited the celebrated fern grottoes.[17] Even with the dense shade, which, however, was somewhat reduced by recent storms, the grottoes showed the effects of the drought. Many of the flowering plants and ferns were wilted. Four tropical shrubs, however, maintained their freshness, and were in both flower and fruit—bird-pepper *(Capsicum baccatum)*, snowberry *(Chiococca alba)*, and wild-coffee *(Psychotria undata, P. sulzneri)*. All these are favorite bird-foods. In this connection, it may be stated that an interesting condition of camouflage was noticed in the case of the rocks and trees. The trees grow on the exposed limestone rock. The large roots of the oaks, the maples, the cypress, and other trees match the weathered limestone rock so closely that it is often difficult to tell, even when only a short distance away, where the roots and the rock meet. Is this a case of protective coloration, or just the harmony so often observed in Nature?

These fern-grottoes are unique. They consist of massive rocks, cliffs, boulders, cañons, wells, and caves, all heavily wooded with cypress trees in the low parts along the Withlacoochee and oaks, maples, hickories and a dozen other kinds of broad-leaved trees. There are sixteen different kinds of ferns flourishing there in profusion. So copious is the growth and intermixed the species that one may frequently grasp the leaves of a half dozen different kinds of ferns in one hand. There are erect ferns, drooping ferns, and creeping ferns on the rocks. The beauty of the fern-growth is augmented by two stemless palms, the needle-palm and the dwarf-palmetto or blue-stem, both of which, contrary to their normal lowland habitat, grow there on the relatively dry rocks. And, all this is in the process of destruction. A large quarry has already defaced one side and further devastation will continue, destroying this unique natural monument.

Traveling from Floral City to Brooksville we were again impressed with the brilliant green of the new leaves of the black-jack *(Quercus catesbaei),* especially when they were contrasted against a background of the live-oak *(Quercus virginiana)* or a screen of pine-trees where they were present. From Brooksville to the Gulf of Mexico scarcely any plants were in bloom, and the effects of the drought had even caused the hardy saw-palmetto *(Serenoa repens)* to turn a decided yellow-green. In the vicinity of Weekiwachee Springs we made two good discoveries, the one the white-leaved gopher-apple *(Geobalanus incanus),* a low shrub with underground stems and mostly confined to the southern part of the peninsula; the other our most showy basil *(Clinopodium coccineum),* a shrub of the mint family with many small leaves and long scarlet flowers nearly or quite two inches in length.

The western Gulf coast from Aripeka to the Pinellas Peninsula had largely recovered from the effect of the hurricane of the preceding fall, but now the drought had it in its grip. Very few plants were in bloom. The almost ubiquitous beggar's-ticks *(Coreopsis leavenworthii)* showed itself here and there, and the native zamia was a conspicuous plant in gardens along the Gulf. We reached Saint Petersburg after dusk and in the morning we went to the west point of Clam Bayou, where we met our four native mangroves—the red, the white, the black, and the button. Among other southern shrubs and trees we found sea-grape *(Coccolobis uvifera),* saffron-plum *(Bumelia angustifolia),* and shrub-lobelia *(Scaevola plumieri).* The most interesting shrub, however, was the large varnish-leaf *(Dodonaea viscosa),* one of our rarest plants. It was found once before in this region and once along Bay Biscayne at Cutler. Two other species of *Dodonaea* occur in Florida, both with smaller leaves and smaller fruits, the one known to occur also in the West Indies, the other endemic on Big Pine Key. One normally subterranean object—here exposed to view by a heavy surf—was of special interest. It was the root and root-stock system of the Spanish-bayonet *(Yucca aloifolia).* This was almost like the corresponding parts of some of the bamboos or greenbriers—species of *Smilax*—from which the aborigines made a red flour.

Another element that reminded us of more tropical regions was the woody coin-vine *(Dalbergia ecastophyllum).* Herbaceous plants were wanting. The shores of Lake Maggiore, however, furnished some herbaceous plants of more northern relationships, such as milkweed *(Asclepias lanceolata),* ladies' tresses *(Ibidium cernuum),* and snakemouth *(Pogonia ophioglossoides).* Yet those two typically southern trees one finds wherever southern birds go, the marlberry *(Icacorea)* and myrsine *(Rapanea),* were present in the hammock.

We next visited Maximo Point where there is a serpentine aboriginal mound running east and west for about a quarter of a mile. Lack of time prevented our investigating this mound. Many stone implements, all imported, of course, by the local aborigines from more northern regions, have been found there.

One of our objects of search was on Long Key. A curiously branching palm, "different from any other found in Florida," had been reported as growing there. Hence we hastened across the bay. Our suspicions had been aroused as to a possible less interesting palm than had been reported, for about Lake Maggiore we had noticed considerable branching among the saw-palmetto plants. The palms on Long Key opposite Gulfport turned out to be the same as those mentioned above. The flora of Long Key as we saw it in December has been described in a former paper.[18] Of course, other plants were noticed at this season than those met with in December. One in particular was a peculiar plant, the whisp-fern *(Psilotum nudum).* This is primarily a hammock inhabitant, but, curiously enough, it occasionally may be found out on exposed sand-dunes growing on the trunks of saw-palmettos and at the bases of other trees.

The next section of the itinerary was a route to the eastern coast. Ponds about Saint Petersburg and Tampa were filled with our largest spatterdock, described some years ago by the writer as *Nymphaea macrophylla.* The leathery leaves sometimes became nearly three feet long and give a pond a rather unusual aspect. The Pinellas Peninsula is of much later development, economically, than the Tampa region, for in the former we find citrus groves and otherwise wild lands; in the latter we find citrus groves and farm-land.

As we entered the lake region, the lowlands showed some flowers on the withe-rod *(Viburnum),* false-asters *(Doellingeria),* beggar's-ticks *(Coreopsis),* pimpernel *(Ilysanthes),* and lobelias. On the sandhills we came upon several places where three dry soil plants were flourishing, and, curiously enough, all three were wand-like plants with the specific name *floridana,* namely, *Eriogonum, Froelichia,* and *Chapmannia.* A coastal plant, the railroad-vine *(Ipomoea pes-capri),* was not uncommon in pinelands. East of Kissimmee we passed out of the lake region into the flat-woods. The lower flats, sparsely populated with pine trees, gave an example of how particular certain plants are as to habitat. Although there was no condition visible to the eye, an area here would be populated with Saint John's-wort *(Hypericum),* another by pitcher-plant *(Sarracenia),* and a contiguous area by a yellow milk-wort *(Polygala).* As a result of seed dispersal there is no reason why the plants should not mix, but the conditions hidden in the soil evidently prevent them from doing so.

From the pinelands we passed into the prairie lagoon of the upper Saint John's River, which stretches from east to west for a distance of about nine miles. The last time we crossed it was a cold December night. This warm spring afternoon was quite a contrast. In spite of the general drought the vast drainage basin supplied the low parts and ditches with water enough to keep the aquatic plants in healthy condition and these *en masse* were wonderful rendezvous for the various water birds. There were colonies of upright aquatics such as cat-tail *(Typha),* wampee *(Pontederia),* arrowhead *(Sagittaria),* violet-flags *(Iris),* with flowers over half a foot wide, and colonies of floating aquatics, such as water-lettuce *(Pistia),* water-hyacinth *(Piaropus),* water-lily *(Castalia),* and spatter-docks *(Nymphaea).* The two latter plants often had leaves that suggested the celebrated "victoria-regia." Water birds of various kinds were standing on or running over the floating colonies of water-plants. The more unusual birds were the Florida-gallinule and the purple-gallinule.

The high pineland eastward, simulating a long ridge viewed from out on the prairie, was soon achieved. The long-leaf pines and the short-leaf ones in the scrub had developed their season's stout twigs just far enough to give the trees the aspect of having been decorated with numerous candles.

As we started down the eastern coast from Melbourne at dusk, the moon-flowers began to burst open all along the way. Later in the evening our spotlight shining several hundred feet ahead brought out the moon-flowers sharply against their dark green backgrounds, and in passing through a hammock we seemed to be passing through an avenue lined with these large, rather unusual, snow-white flowers. After a night at Fort Pierce we pushed on southward. The tropical hammocks along Saint Lucie Sound exhibited fresh anomalies. The more interesting one at this time was the growth of the wild-pepper *(Peperomia humilis).* Here it occupies the highest and driest part of the sand-ridge far from standing water. The rain that does fall rapidly drains into the deep loose sand. In contrast to this phenomenon the habitat of the same species at Cape Sable is semiaquatic—a good part of the year the plants are partly submerged. However, the growth at the two localities is identical in habit and in luxuriance!

The pinelands were usually almost flowerless. Here and there a yellow flower of the big partridge-pea *(Chamaecrista brachiata)* and of a golden-rod *(Solidago)* would appear. The scrub was more interesting, although more desert-like than we had previously seen it. In the virgin scrub the dry weather seemed to bring out the fragrance of the spruce-pine *(Pinus clausa),* which frequently filled the air with a truly spruce-like odor. This fact furnishes a second reason for the popular name of the pine typical of the scrub. The other reason is because the pine in young foliage does resemble a spruce tree when viewed in the landscape.

The result of two methods of destroying scrub were noticed. Where the growth has been removed by clearing the land without burning, the shrubs and pine trees quickly reassert themselves and the scrub tends to be restored. However, when the land has been burned, perhaps repeatedly, the area becomes a sandy waste with few herbaceous plants, and scattered shrubs of a few kinds that spring up from fruits brought in by animals.

Evening found us at Miami with our collecting headquarters established in the laboratory building of the Plant Introduction Garden of the United States Department of Agriculture and at the Charles Deering reservations as well.

Some Hammocks of the Everglade Keys

The time between major excursions was spent in studies particularly in the Deering cactus plantation at Buena Vista, in the Deering hammock at Cutler, and, incidentally, in several of the hammocks of Everglade Keys.[19]

Our first discovery at Cutler was the little West Indian

fern, *Sphenomeris clavata,* in lime-sinks where the pineland formerly met the lowland along Bay Biscayne. About a score of years ago it was discovered this side of the Gulf Stream in a limestone sink a few miles east of the one-time Camp Jackson, then in a sink near the old Silver Palm settlement in the "homestead region," then on a pine island east of Naranja, and finally near the eastern end of Long Pine Key. It was scarce at these localities except the third mentioned one. As soon as we found the fern at Cutler we motored to the big island east of Naranja to see if the fern still grew there. When we first happened on this virgin island, which is fully three miles long and averages a mile in width, it was unspoiled as yet by the white man. Then the rocky floor was literally carpeted with this fern. It grew so luxuriantly that deer would lie in the dense beds and several times they arose from their ferny beds only a few feet in front of us as we approached. This year we found houses nearly everywhere, but not a leaf of the fern! This island had been burned over many times and very likely the fern was thus exterminated. It doubtless met the same fate as in the other localities where it once grew only sparingly, for they lay in the areas of frequent fires.

The prairies about the island had been fire swept so often that very little nourishment remained in the marl. The colicroot *(Aletris),* ladies'-tresses *(Ibidium),* grass-pink *(Limodorum),* yellow-flax *(Cathartolinum),* and marsh-pink *(Sabbatia)* were decorating the prairies with their flowers, but the stunted plants were mostly only about a half foot tall or scarcely a quarter the height their predecessors were wont to be several years before. Once more, it was impressed upon us that tragic truth: Florida is being drained and burned to such an extent that it will soon become a desert! No herbaceous plants had appeared to attract our eye in the high pinelands, but several woody plants had felt the advent of spring—locust-berry *(Byrsonima lucida),* long-stalked stopper *(Anamomis longipes),* coco-plum *(Chrysobalanus pellocarpus),* poison-wood *(Metopium metopium),* darling-plum

(Reynosia septentrionalis), and myrsine *(Rapanea guianensis).* These, however, were not trees as they should have been, but shrubs, with what structures they had developed to correspond to trunks merely gnarled woody masses buried in the erosion holes in the rock. The branches either spread on the surface of the rock or stood up to a height of two or three feet. The moist lime-sinks alone showed color, being often lined with the mist-flower *(Conoclinium)* bearing myriads of diminutive blue brush-like flower heads.

The Hattie Bauer hammock[20] has a number of unique features, and formerly had more. At one time it possessed the finest growth of the West Indian holly *(Ilex krugiana)* this side of the Gulf Stream, and this grove when in flower filled the air with violet-like fragrance far and wide. It excelled all the other hammocks in the number of these trees and also in their size. It is the only locality outside of the West Indies for the rare wild-pepper *(Peperomia spathulifolia).* This plant is represented by a copious and luxuriant growth. It has no close relations in Florida, and is known from only two islands on the other side of the Gulf Stream. The Bauer hammock, too, is the only station for the vine-fern *(Phymatodes exigua)* on the Florida mainland. This little fern, contrary to the usual habit of epiphytes, selects smooth-barked trees for its host or arbor instead of rough-barked ones. The slender stems are flattened in the same plane as the host and are held closely appressed to the bark by numerous rootlets. The young leaves are small, short and broad, and are also appressed to the host. The subsequent leaves, the sporophylls, are long and narrow, and more laxly disposed. This hammock is the home of another noteworthy fern—a fan-shaped filmy one *(Trichomanes punctata).* The sides of some of the large lime-sinks are lined with mats of this little fern—the smallest fern in North America. Its leaves are iridescent and show beautiful shades of green in the half-light of the sinks. The growth of ages clothing the perpendicular honeycombed rock walls, with the leaves overlapping after the manner of a thatch of shingles, may be pulled off in mats, which comprise thousands of leaves. Although the shrubs and trees were quite dilapidated as a result of the protracted drought, the wild-peppers and the ferns just referred to were thriving luxuriantly. Many kinds of ferns occupy appropriate habitats in the Bauer hammock, both terrestrial and epiphytic. Four kinds of halberd-fern *(Tectaria)* occur there. In fact, it is the only hammock where all four species grow, and two of them are endemic. The interesting phenomenon in this connection was some plants of the small halberd-fern *(Tectaria minima)* "sporting," *i.e.,* the leaf-blades were irregularly cut beyond the normal incisions, after the manner of some forms of the Boston-fern *(Nephrolepis).*

The Nixon-Lewis hammock likewise is a rich botanical repository. Another kind of filmy-fern *(Trichomanes krausii)* has its home there—a feather-shaped filmy fern unlike the one referred to above. This kind inhabits tree-trunks and prostrate logs, instead of rocks. More showy than the fern is one of the many kinds of epiphytic orchids. This is the large spider-orchid *(Brassia caudata),* and the long strings of spider-like, mottled flowers hung in clusters from the limbs of trees. This is the only hammock in the Biscayne pineland where Brassia grows.

The air was fragrant with the odors of various blooming shrubs that grew about the margins of the hammocks. The bustic or cassada *(Dipholis salicifolia)* gave off an odor resembling cherry blossoms or sometimes trailing arbutus, while the fragrance of the rough velvet-seed *(Guettarda scabra)* resembled that of the Japanese honeysuckle *(Nintooa japonica).*

From Miami we went on to Cape Sable.[21] Three days were devoted to the region of the Cape with instructive results and where much of interest still remains to be disclosed. There were two outstanding phenomena observed en route in the Biscayne Pineland. The one the occurrence of the cypress *(Taxodium)* in the hammocks on the southern side of Snapper Creek prairie. This is the only locality one finds for the cypress south of the Miami River until the Royal Palm hammock is reached. The cypress was formerly well represented in the hammocks where the prairie and the Everglades met. These were favorite temporary camping places for the Indians. The growth culminates in the Deering Snapper Creek hammock, where it is plentiful, and nearly reaches the coastal salt marshes. The other phenomenon is the growth of poison-wood trees *(Metopium)* in the pinewoods west of Big Hammock prairie. These trees represent the sole arboreous growth in the pinewoods other than pine trees and form striking objects with their pale-gray bark and deep green leaves.

As a result of the long drought the water-table of the Everglades was very low. The ditches along the highway about Royal Palm hammock were dry—a condition heretofore not often observed. As we proceeded southward beyond Royal Palm hammock, water began to appear in the ditch along the roadway and for many miles it increased in depth in proportion as the land decreased in altitude, until the region of the influence of the tide was reached. There, of course, the depth of the water depended upon the state of the tide of the Bay of Florida. Various ponds on the Lossman's River limestone, which were ordinarily filled with water, and were now dry or only partly filled, depended on the state of the tide. The soft mud of these ponds was marked with the tracks of heavy saurians, evidently of two kinds, perhaps those of alligators and of crocodiles. For some distance southwest of Royal Palm hammock a tropical flea-bane *(Pluchea odorata)* had taken possession of the side of the highway. This plant was known to grow on Key West for many years before it spread elsewhere in Florida. With the advent of the railroad on the Keys, the fruits were carried eastward to other Keys. The prevailing wind then evidently carried the fruits, which are constructed for wind transportation, northeastward. Several years ago the plant was discovered on the prairies east of Homestead, and now they appeared below Royal Palm hammock. The new verdure of early spring was evident everywhere. The fresh leaves of the hundreds of hammocks clothing the little rock reefs on the Miami oölite not only showed different tints according to the species, but also according to the elevation of the sun and the consequent angles of its rays. The cypress trees both within the heads and on the prairies showed a vivid green of leaves, instead of the ghastly white of the bark of a few months previous. Many of the marshes of the Lossman's River limestone were covered with a dense growth of a dark-green or brownish rush *(Juncus roemerianus),* or a sedge *(Mariscus jamaicensis),* light-green when young or simulating a field of fire when its tall flowering panicles were pushed up above the leaves.

A Prehistoric Canal at Cape Sable

We drove to the crossing of the old Flamingo-Coot Bay trail, then proceeded afoot westward on the embankment of marl thrown up by the dredge in excavating the canal. Canals dug by man are not new to that part of the country. There was one dug there through the marl ages ago by the aborigines. It is true that the channel is mostly filled in, but in periods of the greatest drought the former ditch is always wet. Thus its vegetation differs from that in the region through which it runs. The natural growth is less dense and ferns do not grow there, as the soil is too continuously wet. There seems no doubt as to the aboriginal origin of this water-way, for all the natural canals of the region, for example those connecting the various lakes, remain open and their banks are devoid of aboriginal activities. The canal that is now filled in has small kitchen-middens on its banks. These consist mostly of the shells of the oyster, clam, and conch. The position of the old canal can be seen where the embankment of the Ingraham Highway crosses it running westward, and where the Roberts Highway[22] crosses it running southward to the settlement of Flamingo. The embankment of the highways continues to settle after that on either side has become firm, and the water by capillary attraction rises to the surface and makes the roadway boggy.

By means of this artificial channel, the aborigines could pass in a few miles from the Whitewater Bay region through Coot Bay into Mud Lake, by a natural channel, and thence to the Bay of Florida, thus saving a distance of fifty miles, more or less, and perhaps, a rough trip around Cape Sable, where by a combined action of winds and tides very rough water may result. This gave them a short cut and a protected water passage to the Florida Keys, where some of their people had settlements, as described in this narrative under the excursion to Big Pine Key. The successors of the aborigines also made a short cut across the Cape Sable region. In calm weather they rounded the Cape in going from the Ten Thousand Islands to the Florida Keys. But in stormy weather they took their canoes into Whitewater Bay as far as the most southern shore, and then carried or dragged them over a trail for a distance of about five miles to the shores of Florida Bay, about midway between the present settlement of Flamingo and the East Cape.

Aboriginal Activities at Cape Romano

A week was devoted to one of our major excursions, the ultimate objective being Cape Romano. The necessary course was still a long detour around the head of Lake Okeechobee. The distance of our objective made haste desirable, and consequently little collecting was done along the eastern coastal region. However, in driving northward along the beach, the various shades of green were impressed upon us. With the background of the indigo Gulf Stream and the paler-blue cloudless sky above the sharply defined horizon, the silver-green of the saw-palmetto *(Serenoa repens),* the gray-green of the beach-heliotrope *(Tournefortia gnaphaloides),* the yellow-green of the bay-cedar *(Suriana maritima)* were all strongly emphasized. Inland the color of flowers, varying with the season and rainfall, was impressed on us by the yellow-heliotrope *(Heliotropium leavenworthii),* which was more golden than we had noticed it previously. West of the Jupiter River and its tributaries the usually subaqueous Hungry Land[23] was nearly dry. Even the robust Peruvian evening-primrose *(Jussiaea peruviana)* was unable to produce flowers more than an inch in diameter, which is less than half the usual size.

There was little to attract the eye in the way of color and, curiously enough, the color of flowers that were present was uniformly yellow. Former ponds were turned into pygmy forests, the tiny trees being the sand-weed *(Hypericum fasciculatum).* They were suggestive of miniature cypress trees. Grassy places supported a trinity of yellow milkworts *(Polygala cymosa, P. ramosa, P. lutea).* The yellow bladderwort *(Stomoisia juncea)* grew along with the white-top *(Dichromena latifolia)* which over-topped it with its clustered inflorescence.

The desert-like areas of sand pumped from the Saint Lucie slough[24] seemed dry as dust, yet they supported some vegetation, consisting mainly of such hardy herbs as wormwood *(Chenopodium ambrosioides),* switch-grass *(Spartina bakeri),* Bermuda-grass *(Capriola dactylon),* and beggar's-ticks *(Bidens leucantha).* The shores of the Saint Lucie canal had lately become lined with the Peruvian evening primrose *(Jussiaea peruviana),* and so luxuriant is the growth in some places that the plants have assumed the habit of small trees.

On the western side of the canal we met a motor car with the engine almost burning. When asked in what condition the thirty odd miles of trail to Lake Okeechobee were, the driver replied: "The trail is pretty good if you can get over it." With this information we set out.

Near the Saint Lucie slough the swamp-bracken *(Blechnum serrulatum)* was at its best and formed vast areas of light green. Farther on, along the borders where the pinelands end and the prairies meet, the ground was a mass of fluffy gray as a result of the numerous fruiting heads of the pine-hyacinth *(Viorna baldwinii)* and the pine-thistle *(Cirsium smallii).* We ran out to the lake about sixteen miles south of its head and drove up to the present shore which a few years ago was the bottom of the lake. Lines of guava shrubs or groundsel bush indicated the former stages of the water. The seeds of the guava from which these bushes spring were washed down from the hammock-ridge and sprouted in lines where lodged; the fruits of the groundsel-bush were blown into the lake and washed ashore in lines where they, too, took root. The old natural shore-line was indicated by the ragged fringed hammock, often only marked by a solitary cabbage-tree of a group, for these plants are more immune to fire than any of the other elements of the vegetation. The height of the water of the lake during recent westerly storms was indicated by the dead plant of the water-hyacinth *(Piaropus crassipes)* heaped up in lines on the sand.

Early the following morning we continued our journey, starting out from Okeechobee City. This time we forsook the old trail to the Cabbage Bluff and the Caloosahatchee, and decided on a more fascinating route, namely, that over the recently exposed bottom of the western side of Lake Okeechobee. As we started down the lake bottom south of Okeechobee City we drove through acres of poke-weed *(Phytolacca rigida),* false-nettle *(Boehmeria cylindrica),* and vervain *(Verbena polystachya),* each of which had taken possession of the land often in almost pure growths. We were soon in Eagle Bay, as indicated by the extensive marshes in which we promptly bogged. About an hour was consumed in digging the car out of the mud, after which we crossed a stretch of water, which fortunately had a hard sand bottom just about where we had anchored with a forty-five foot cruiser nearly ten years before. The marshes of Eagle Bay were vast fields of water-hyacinth *(Piaropus crassipes)* and giant arrow-head *(Sagittaria lancifolia),* whose constantly decaying parts, together with the remains of the vegetation that preceded them, formed a deep layer of black humus over the sandy or flat rock foundation. Between Eagle Bay and the mouth of the Kissimmee River the very gently sloping lake bottom was barren of vegetation, except clumps of very tall pickerel-weed *(Pontederia cordata),* which, on a small scale, resembled the hammock islands of the Everglade-prairie near the Bay of Florida. Further on, vegetation became more abundant and such pioneer herbs as smart-weed *(Persicaria),* false-nettle *(Boehmeria),* fire-weed *(Erechtites),* and dog-fennel *(Eupatorium)* monopolized nearly all the land the lake had recently given up. Upon limited areas even woody plants had invaded; thus we noticed willow *(Salix),* groundsel-bush *(Baccharis),* and even saw-palmetto *(Serenoa)* and cypress *(Taxodium).* The growth of baccharis was often so dense and luxuriant that it formed an almost impassable barrier. In dry sloughs the water-hyacinth had given way to the amphibious smart-weed *(Persicaria).* Thence for several miles the prairie-like bottom gradually rose to more elevated stretches.

While hunting for the trail which we temporarily lost several miles east and south of the mouth of Fisheating Creek, we were surprised to find three Indian mounds of sand which, when the waters of the lake stood at normal height, were perhaps several miles off shore. The mounds were of different sizes and their vegetation was limited in variety and different from the vegetation of the nearest former shores. The herb present was poor-man's patches *(Mentzelia).* There were three kinds of trees present: the dahoon or yaupon *(Ilex cassine),* the wax-myrtle *(Cerothamnus ceriferus),* and the sugar-berry *(Celtis missis-*

sippiensis). The latter were big trees, descendants, of course, of those that were there during the aboriginal occupation. However, the aborigines have been absent only between one and two centuries, and it may be that the sugar-berry is not there by accident. For, it being a deciduous-leaved tree of rather rapid growth, the red man who occupied these sites could have had the benefit of the cool shade in summer and the warmth of the sun in the winter. A little further on we came upon another very large mound, located at a township stake, 41 south, and range 32 east. Most of the arboreous growth of this mound had been destroyed by fire. A few cypress trees and ash trees remained. The castor-bean *(Ricinus communis),* however, had taken possession of a large area and grew luxuriantly. The plants were in both flower and fruit, and while we were on the mound the car was continually pelted with the seeds thrown in all directions from the explosive capsules. We soon found the trail, and further on found the advance guard of civilization constructing a canal and a road leading to the local metropolis of Moorehaven. On a previous page we remarked about how the aborigines piled up vast quantities of shells, unknowingly, of course, ready for the white man to turn into roads. Here nature had prepared for the same step in civilization. The superficial geological structure here is a layer of humus on top of about six feet of sand, and then a deep layer of shells. To make the canal is merely to excavate. The hard road is a result of the excavation, *i.e.,* the geological strata are reversed; the sand is thrown up on the prairie—lately the lake bottom—to make an embankment, and the shells from the layer beneath are placed on top of the sand to make a hard surfaced road. Our approach to modern civilization was also indicated by the sight of vast areas of sandy prairies with a thin coating of red dust, which was the only remains of the thick layer of humus that had been slowly laid down by nature through the ages, and only recently been burned off.

Our visit to this region, about six years ago, was

described in two papers printed in 1918.[25] The remarkable fertility of the humus where it remained was still evident, but the widespread destruction continued and was shown by the vast desert of white sand where formerly a jungle was supported on a deep humus-deposit. Where this deposit remained either cultivated crops abounded or the original hammocks and the forests of elder *(Sambucus simpsonii)* were emphasized in the landscape.

Native and exotic grasses grow with remarkable luxuriance in the humus: the switch-grass *(Spartina bakeri),* the panic-grass *(Panicum bartowense),* the Bermuda-grass *(Capriola dactylon),* the Rhodes-grass *(Chloris gayana),* and the finger-grass *(Eustachys glauca)* all grew to nearly twice their usual size.

The remarkable vitality of the arrowhead *(Sagittaria lancifolia)* was illustrated by a growth of that plant, whose habitat is in water or about on the water-table, on dry sand banks thrown up six to ten feet above the natural surface of the prairie. With it grew, naturalized, the dasheen *(Colocasia antiquorum),* with its tubers buried deep in the sand. Another naturalized plant of the region is a bushy potato *(Solanum torvum),* which is thoroughly established in several widely separated places. The only conspicuous native plant then in bloom was the thistle *(Cirsium smallii),* which acted somewhat as a fire-weed, often giving the distant burned or partly burned areas a rose-purple tint with its myriad flower heads.

Traveling westward from Moorehaven, the boundary of the prairie appeared as a continuous blue line on the horizon. Our approach to the edge of the prairie was indicated by the appearance of saw-palmetto *(Serenoa repens)* and gall-berry *(Ilex glabra).* There the saw-palmetto was in bloom and the flowers gave off the odor of coumerin. After traveling for fourteen or fifteen miles, the blue line of the horizon, mentioned above, broke up into patches of pineland, hammock, and cabbage-tree clusters, all indicative of the water-shed of the Caloosahatchee. There the flora changed. The drought had, evidently, so much reduced the pasturage that cattle had taken to eating the leaves of the saw-palmetto, just as they are accustomed to browse on the dwarf-palmetto *(Sabal minor)* when it is available. The flora was not showy. A beggar's-ticks *(Coreopsis leavenworthii)* was the most conspicuous plant and a queen's-delight *(Stillingia spatulata)* grew with it. Of more interest were two of our small and inconspicuous plants—a water-starwort *(Callitriche nuttallii),* whose foliage gives off the fragrance of sweet-vernal grass in drying, and an equally small plant, the chaffweed *(Centunculus pentandrus).* These are carpet-plants. They delight in the margins of ponds, and as the water dries up they follow it as it recedes, covering the muck with often a complete green surface.

The long drought had been broken on the western coast by heavy showers a few days previous to our advent. Consequently, the belated vegetation awoke with a rush. At least two dozen kinds of flowers, representing nearly as many natural plant families, grew along the way from Fort Myers to Naples.

Recently fire-swept pinelands, bare otherwise, were here and there embellished with patches of pine-hyacinth *(Viorna baldwinii)* and pine-lily *(Atamosco simpsonii),* whose subterranean food-reservoirs seem to be stimulated to activity by fire sweeping over them. There again, far from any habitation, we found the guava growing naturally. Before crossing to Marco Island we drove into the Royal Palm hammocks[26] in spite of forest fires which swept across the trail in several places, and threatening thunderstorms which would have made the prairie impassable, had they deluged the land with their rains. After passing the palm hammock strand, consisting of cypress *(Taxodium),* cabbage-trees *(Sabal),* maple *(Acer),* and sweet-bay *(Magnolia),* the tops of numerous royal-palms appeared both to the east and to the west. On the trunks of these palms the rare Cuban orchid *(Polyrrhiza lindenii)* was first found this side of the Gulf Stream. It is a curious plant, consisting mainly of cord-like roots, as the generic name indicates, from which a short almost leafless stem arises, which in turn bears a large white, butterfly-like flower and then a long fruit somewhat resembling a small "vanilla bean."

Vegetation in these hammocks is exceedingly vigorous. For example, the gamma-grass *(Tripsacum)* and the plume-grass *(Erianthus)* grew twice as high as one's head. The Blodgett-potato *(Solanum blodgettii),* which usually is under three feet in height, also grew up to twelve feet high. In the open places there were fields of dye-plant *(Flaveria)* and great clumps of germander *(Teucrium)* and its relative the obedient-plant *(Dracocephalum).* The greatest surprise, however, was the finding of the Australian-pine *(Casuarina)* which had sprung up in the jungle, perhaps, from seeds blown all the way across the peninsula, by stages, of course, from the numerous trees on the opposite eastern coast.

The general destruction referred to on previous and succeeding pages was emphasized by increasing forest fires in various directions. The smoke and flame, together with the clouds of local thunderstorms, gave the outlook a lurid tinge. Fortunately, we got back to the sandy trail just as a storm burst and made the marl prairie so slippery that a motor car could not have traversed it. A drive to Marco Pass, a ferry cross it, and a drive across Marco Island, brought us to our destination, namely, Caxambas.[27]

Although there were no signs of ancient Indian occupation in the Royal-Palm hammocks, the aboriginal red man doubtless derived part of his sustenance from the copious fruits of the palms.

On the other hand, Marco Island and Caxambas Island furnish ample evidence of their activities, and furthermore these Royal-Palm hammocks were easily reached by water in former times, just as they are now. There is a large kitchen-midden at the northern end of Marco Island where the modern town of Marco has sprung up, while a very large midden—over several hundred acres in extent—occupies a kind of broad swale between the sandhills at the southern end of

Caxambas Island. Here is the settlement of Caxambas. It is interesting to note how the white man has so often unconsciously selected the old village sites of the red man for his modern towns and cities. The Marco midden produced little of interest, except a ground cover of Dr. Garber's potato *(Boerhaavia coccinea)* with myriads of little purple flowers and wild-cotton *(Gossypium punctatum)* with large flowers, white in the morning and pink in the afternoon.

The southerly tip of Romano Island is Cape Romano, our ultimate goal. The object of our search was the thatch-palm *(Thrinax parviflora),* which has been reported as growing there, having been discovered in that region in 1876.[28] Our search was not rewarded by success; in fact, some of the older residents of the region, who have been acquainted with the palms of the Florida Keys and of Cape Sable, claim that this palm had never been found on Cape Romano to the best of their knowledge.

However, even if this thatch-palm did not grow on Cape Romano, it evidently occurred and may still exist in that region. In addition to the Chapman record, which merely reads, "Coast and Keys of South Florida," specimens are extant said to have been collected on "Caximbas Island, Florida, April 26, 1892, by J. H. Simpson." Since writing the above, the following information was received in a letter from Captain John F. Horr, who is the best informed man on the history of the region under consideration. Referring to both the name Caxambas and the palm in question, he says:

"I always understood the word means wells, or springs. Cuban fishing smacks often filled their casks with fresh water there. If I understand the palm problem, the Thrinax is the little palm, of which there were a few on Cape Romano in 1875. I think the turtlers of Key West who used to come there for green-turtle used them to make their crawls, to confine the turtle until ready to go back to Key West. I know of no palms of that kind near the cape now."

Cape Romano and the island it is on is an isolated

place—well out in the Gulf of Mexico. Most of the island is low, but an elevated barrier ridge extends along the western, southern, and eastern sides. Much of this ridge consists of small shells piled up by the surf, similar to the dunes on the islands off the Pinellas Peninsula—all suggesting, in connection with the very prolific flowering and fruiting of many plants, the prodigious wastefulness of nature. Mangroves, the four different kinds, occupied the low land of the cape. The sand and shell ridges supported a high hammock growth. A dozen kinds of shrubs and trees of a tropical character were common. Among them were sea-grape *(Coccolobis),* bay-cedar *(Suriana),* stopper *(Eugenia),* Jamaica-dogwood *(Ichthyomethia),* cat's-claw *(Pithecolobium),* snowberry *(Chiococca).* Herbs were scarce, a condition doubtless due to the frequent flooding of the ridge during storms. The rail-road-vine *(Ipomoea pes-capri),* dew-flower *(Commelina angustifolia)* and sea-rocket *(Cakile lanceolata)* were the only common kinds of herbaceous plants in evidence.

Although the palm we sought was not forthcoming, the palm family was copiously represented by the cabbage-tree *(Sabal)* and the saw-palmetto *(Serenoa).* The cabbage-tree harbored the sole representative of the fern family, the epiphytic serpent-fern *(Phlebodium).*

The advent of new foliage was on and the shades of green were numerous. In addition to green, the developing leaves of the often quite symmetrical wind-pruned gumbo-limbo *(Elaphrium)* and the irregular cat's-claw *(Pithecolobium)* and sea-grape *(Coccolobis)* showed various shades of red.

The beach-ridge, not conducive to the growth of tender plants, was evidently suited to the more rugged cacti. Prickly-pears *(Opuntiae)* were plentiful and of as many shades of green as there were species, and, in addition, the dildoe *(Acanthocereus floridanus),* sprawled over the shrubbery. The striped-spined prickly-pear *(Opuntia zebrina),* not before known north of Cape Sable, was, perhaps, the dominant species. The tropical *Opuntia dillenii* was represented and also a relative with much longer and relatively more slender straight spines—*Opuntia ochrocentra* which also grows on Big Pine Key. The kinds so far mentioned are erect plants. More interesting, however, was a smaller prostrate kind, with a pale-green hue and short clustered white spines. Its flower is small, with triangular sepals and few narrow petals. The young fruits, too, indicate something different from that of our other known species of Opuntia.[29] Another striking succulent on the sand-ridges was the century-plant *(Agave decipiens)* which simulated the Spanish-bayonet *(Yucca)* in habit. The leafy stems stood often higher than one's head.

Romano Island was not in favor with the aborigines as a place of residence. At least, there are no evidences of its having been occupied in any permanent way. However, the island between that and Marco Island, Horr's Island, named for Captain Horr mentioned above, tells a quite different history. There the sand-dunes are higher and the still higher kitchen-middens indicate much former aboriginal activity. Sand-dunes alone occupy the western part of the island; on the eastern part and facing the north, is a series of high shell-mounds which fall off abruptly into Caxambas Bay. At the eastern end there is said to be a burial mound. While collecting on the westernmost shell-mound, we came upon the old fire-place where the aborigines evidently cooked such foods as they did not eat raw. The flora of the middens is mainly woody and much more interesting than that of the nearby Cape Romano. In addition to the woody plants, mentioned in connection with the cape, we found on the shell-mound such tropical shrubs and trees as: chaparral-shrub *(Momisia),* strangling-fig *(Ficus),* devil's-claws *(Pisonia),* caper-tree *(Capparis),* coin-vine *(Dalbergia),* coco-plum *(Chrysobalanus),* soapberry *(Sapindus),* marlberry *(Icacorea),* myrsine *(Rapanea),* heliotrope-vine *(Tournefortia),* hog-plum *(Ximenia),* wild-coffee *(Psychotria),* fire-bush *(Hamelia)*—all interesting in being bearers of bird-carried fruits. The lime *(Citrus spinosissima)* was also there, perhaps a relic of aboriginal occupation after the advent of the Spaniards.

The coconut *(Cocos nucifera)* is hardy on Horr's Island. There are many good specimens on the island planted by Captain Horr in 1884.

The shell-middens at Caxambas, opposite Horr's Island, are somewhat peculiar in that they consist largely of conch shells. They support a very forbidding plant covering—century plants *(Agave decipiens),* prickly-pears *(Opuntiae),* dildoes *(Acanthocereus floridanus),* and armed rigid shrubs, as the hog-plum *(Ximenia americana),* the cat's-claw *(Pithecolobium unguis-cati),* wild-lime *(Zanthoxylum fagara),* and sprawling vines, as the devil's-claws *(Pisonia aculeata),* gray-nicker *(Guilandina crista).*

The middens are very interesting, both as to their contents and their floristics. It must have been the scene of wonderful activities in ancient times. The accumulation of conch shells is prodigious, and each one was punctured in the same way for the purpose of removing the animal for eating. In the perpendicular sections made by digging away the shells for making roads, layers or strata of different kinds of shells may be seen. These indicate the remains of the eating during different seasons or of different occupations. Also, marking off different strata are layers of charcoal and bones of animals which indicate where the animals were cooked and eaten. In addition to the large midden, there is a small one in the mangroves. This, as in the case of the village site and burial mound in the mangroves along Bay Biscayne, referred to on a subsequent page, may once have been on higher ground. It may furnish another bit of evidence that the Coastal Plain is slowly sinking. Various stone implements have been found in these middens, imported, of course, from further north. For example, recently found among the shells was a circular millstone about a foot and a half in diameter with an eccentric hole, evidently for a handle. It was doubtless used for grinding palm seeds and perhaps maize. Two beautifully finished ceremonial ax-heads of granite or syenite have been unearthed. The woody and succulent vegetation on the midden and sandhills was flourishing, but the long drought had rendered them a desert as far as herbaceous vegetation was concerned.

The lime of the disintegrating shells, the humus from past vegetation, the slowly decomposing bones, and the charcoal furnish an ideal food for many plants, for the surface of the midden is copiously clothed with vegetation. Many giant live-oaks and other trees lay prostrate as a result of the digging away of the shell-mass. One tree among those fallen and those still standing was the coral-bean *(Erythrina arborea).* This woody plant grows as a vine, a shrub, and a tree. On these shell-middens it occurred as a tree and a shrub combined. It grew just as the Jamaica-dogwood *(Ichthyomethia)* does on the southern front of Big Pine Key, as described on a subsequent page. Several stems or trunks, six to ten together, arose from the ground. The bark, too, was smooth and green, just as in the dogwood.

The sand dunes near the kitchen-middens are of especial botanical interest. The prickly-pear *(Opuntia polycarpa),* so abundant at Atlantic Beach east of Jacksonville, is repeated here both in kind and in abundance. The existence of these two cactus fields at diagonally opposite ends of the Florida peninsula gives some grounds for considering the present cactus flora of the State a remnant of a former wider and more abundant growth of these succulents. There we found the giant-rooted morning-glory *(Ipomoea macrorhiza),* previously seen on the shell-middens along Crystal River, also, with roots large enough to fill a bushel-basket. A very slender spurge *(Chamaesyce)* was plentiful on the bare sands, but usually almost invisible on account of the color of the stems and leaves which closely match that of the sand. Upon examination some plants showed as many as two dozen stems radiating from one root. The sisal *(Agave rigida)* has been naturalized on these dunes for a long time and grew in close association with the native *A. decipiens.*

Where the normal plant-covering of the dunes had been burned off, a rampant growth of vines covered the ground—

green-brier *(Smilax),* milk-pea *(Galactia),* and muscadine-grape *(Muscadinia)* were intertwined over large areas, often acres in extent.

A Detour Across the Peninsula

While returning through Fort Myers we visited a specimen of the cannon-ball tree *(Couroupita guianensis),* said to be the only specimen in continental North America. This is a large widely branching tree, but the flowers and fruits are borne along the main trunk. The showy flowers have a very irregular stamen development, and the globose woody-shelled fruits, about six inches in diameter, hang down along the trunk until they fall to the ground, where they burst with a loud report, and give off the unpleasant odor characteristic of the skunk.

From Fort Myers we set out towards the eastern coast by way of the head of Lake Okeechobee. After crossing the Caloosahatchee at La Belle we headed over the prairies for the settlement of Palmdale. Heavy thunderstorms surrounded us on all sides and we pushed on rapidly. It was interesting to notice how, as we advanced on the prairie, leaving the Caloosahatchee valley, the saw-palmettos *(Serenoa)* gradually lost stature and vigor, until we reached the influence of Fisheating Creek—where they gradually increased in size and were often accompanied by colonies of a tall bear-grass *(Yucca filamentosa).*

As the night was dark and stormy, we decided to stop at Palmdale instead of pushing on over the roadless prairie to Okeechobee City.[30] The prairie is not trackless, for there are trails and innumerable branch trails, nearly all of which looked alike, especially at night, and in a stormy night one is almost sure to get on a wrong trail.

The weather conditions had changed after the thunderstorms of the evening. In the morning a heavy fog was spread over the prairie and remained dense until eight o'clock. We groped our way over the forking trails north of Palmdale until we found the one leading to the Kissimmee River ford at Cabbage Bluff. Little vegetation was in bloom on the prairie and what there was seemed more stunted than usual. The plants, often in large patches, of pine-hyacinth *(Viorna),* blue-hearts *(Buchnera),* heliotrope *(Heliotropium),* tread-softly *(Cnidoscolus),* black-root *(Pterocaulon),* and marsh-fleabane *(Pluchea)* varied mostly from two to six inches in height. The curious areas of white quick-sand in the midst of the prairies, usually destitute of vegetation, perhaps on account of the alternating wet and dry conditions, were at this time real deserts. Usually there are scattered plants of bladderwort and sedges to be seen at least about their margins.

The characteristic dominant vegetation of this prairie, however, is the palm. The cabbage-tree *(Sabal)* and the saw-palmetto *(Serenoa)* form hundreds of oases comprising a single plant or colonies of hundreds or thousands. As we approached the edge of this palm growth, the isolated cabbage trees veiled in the fog resembled the smoke arising from so many Indian camp fires. With the myriad of these two kinds of palms intimately associated, first a fact and then a question impressed themselves on us: the pistils of the palm of one genus are perfectly sterile to the pollen of the other, for there is never any sign of hybridization between the species. The question is why does the cabbage-tree have an erect trunk while the saw-palmetto has not only a prostrate but a creeping trunk?

We did run into several large Indian villages further on, but their fires were not burning. The whole population of several villages had recently left, evidently to attend their annual council and ceremonial green-corn dance. These villages occupy cabbage-tree groves. This palm furnishes the red man with most of the necessities and some of the luxuries—material for construction, fuel, food, just as the screw-pine serves the native of some parts of the East Indies.

Extensive fires had swept not only the prairie, but many of the palm oases, leaving them in a deplorable state from which it will take a long time for restoration to their normal condition. Towards the northern side of the prairie, as well as near the southern side, we found the guava *(Psidium guajava)* thoroughly naturalized. From the edge of the prairie to the Kissimmee River prairie, pine trees and saw-palmetto occupy the higher land. On the eastern side of the river the open prairie merges into a growth of scattered pine-trees, cabbage-trees, and islands of saw-palmetto. This growth in turn gives way to high pineland, which divides the Kissimmee prairies from the Okeechobee prairies.

The next morning we drove down the eastern side of Lake Okeechobee on the former lake bottom, as far as what used to be Chancy Bay. Toward the bay and the former channel leading into it was dry land. The low stage of the water revealed the indications of several former shore lines of recent geologic time. The fluctuation of the lake during the last decade was indicated by different lines of weed-like growth of dog-fennel *(Eupatorium capillifolium),* fire-weed *(Erechtites hieracifolia),* and mallow *(Kosteletzkya althaeifolia).*

Here we were again very forcibly impressed with the terrible destruction which is returning Florida to its primitive geological condition, namely, a barren desert. DRAINAGE and FIRE! The two processes are tending to eliminate all native life from the State. We made incursions into the remains of the old marginal hammock of the lake. This hammock has been referred to both in its virgin condition[31] and after it had been ravaged by the axe and by fire.[32] The wanton destruction continues! We walked through the skeleton of the hammock. The once deep humus was gone. In its place white sand met the eye. Even the ashes of the humus had been washed away. Some of the giant cypress trees *(Taxodium distichum)* were prostrate, some were standing, either dead or alive, but only to emphasize the almost complete destruction! Where the root-systems of the big cypress trees were once buried in several feet of humus so spongy that one could walk in it only with difficulty, not a bit of humus remained. The root-systems, with their accompanying "knees," stood anchored only in sand, and one could crawl or even walk through the network of once subterranean branched roots. Thus the magnificent monument that took ages to construct has been wrecked within the fraction of a generation!

Still with every necessity gone, the shade of the big trees and humus and its fungi for nourishment, the hammock shrubs and herbs seem to strive to replace their progenitors. But the result is pitiable—puny bits of growth of ferns and herbs here and there in place of masses impenetrable, except by the aid of a machete. The wild-coffee *(Psychotria sulzneri)* seems to be the only native shrub that is equal to the occasion. Here and there a citrus tree—orange or lemon—stands out to remind one of the aboriginal occupation of that one-time Eden. These trees, the descendants of those brought into Florida by the Spanish invaders shortly after the discovery of the Western World, and an occasional almost obliterated burial mound of the aborigines, alone indicate the last stand of the aboriginal red man in that region.

Referring to the Okeechobee country, Hernando de Escalante Fontaneda records that:[33]

"On this lake [Lake of Mayaimi, now Lake Okeechobee], which lies in the midst of the country, are many towns, although of not more than thirty or forty souls each; and as many more places there are in which people are not so numerous. The inhabitants make bread of roots, which is their common food the greater part of the year; and because of the lake, which rises in some seasons so high that the roots cannot be reached in consequence of the water, they are for some time without eating this bread. Fish is plenty and very good. There is another root, like the truffle of this country, which is sweet; and there are other different roots of many kinds...."

The "roots" referred to are the underground parts of the

coontie *(Zamia),* the china-brier *(Smilax),* and the groundnut *(Glycine apios).*

Had Lake Okeechobee been accessible to the advancing white man at an earlier date than it was, this devastation just referred to would have occurred earlier. The surrounding country, more or less, occupied from the first half of the last century, was ruined long ago. The woods and prairies once maintained a growth of scrub oaks and other food plants which fed an abundance of native animals, as well as semi-wild hogs and cattle. The prairies and pine woods have been burned over so much that their former growth of animal foods has disappeared, and as a consequence the native animals have disappeared. The half-wild domestic animals live in a half-starved condition, but their numbers have been reduced by fires in the humus. Driven to seek food in the humus regions, which are often afire for long periods beneath the surface, the hogs and cattle fall through the superficial crust only to have their feet burned off in the fire beneath. They consequently perish. Drainage and burning has become such a fad or even a mania in Florida that the land will soon be unable to support vegetable life, which in turn supports animal life!

A Cruise Among the Florida Keys

After leaving the lake we proceeded at once to our headquarters in Miami.

As soon as we returned from the Cape Romano region we set out for the Florida Keys. Our first stop was on Long Key,[34] made for the purpose of visiting the grove of buccaneer-palms *(Pseudophoenix vinifera),* which was discovered there nearly a half century ago.[35] The grove is situated on a small plateau of sand and is protected from the ocean by a barrier ridge and a swamp. Where there were several hundred palms a generation ago, only about two dozen remain. The grove has been plundered almost to the extent of wiping it off the island. There is much variation in the habit of growth of the trunks of the few trees that remain. Some are nearly cylindric, others are strongly spindle-shaped. There were twin palm trees. The fruit of the buccaneer-palm consists of the ripened gynoecium with one, or two, or three carpels, thus containing one, or two, or three seeds. One fruit with two seeds had sprouted and the result was two palms with the trunks so close together at the base that they looked as if they came from the same root. If a seed with three carpels had sprouted and continued to grow, there would have been triplets. Perhaps some such specimens existed in the original grove. The trees associated with the palm and forming the hammock were poison-wood *(Metopium),* stopper *(Eugenia),* wild-dilly *(Mimusops),* and black-bead *(Pithecolobium).* After securing some photographs of the palms we proceeded to Big Pine Key.

Big Pine Key[36] is a wonderful botanical region. Although only a few—eight—square miles in extent each successive incursion discovers plants of particular interest, and even novelties. We sailed along the front of Big Pine to Newfound Harbor Keys, which represents the same geologic formation as the southern front of Big Pine, but unfavorable weather prevented our landing there. We returned to the lower end of No Name Channel and landed on Big Pine, where we walked along the southern front westward to the channel that separates Big Pine from Newfound Harbor Keys. Darkness was upon us, but we obtained a good idea of this formerly unvisited part of the island. The ubiquitous herb was the mosquito-plant *(Ocimum micranthum)* which filled the air with its spicy fragrance and the likewise abundant woody plant, scarcely to be called a tree here, was the Jamaica-dogwood *(Ichthyomethia).* Every specimen we saw was branched at the base after the manner of the pop-ash

(Fraxinus).[37] There were no plants with single stems. Just what this condition signifies we are not prepared to say. The Jamaica-dogwood was in all stages of development: there were plants with only flowers, plants with only fruits, plants with flowers and leaves, plants with fruits and leaves, and finally plants with leaves, flowers, and fruits—another inexplicable variation.

On the shell-ridge between the beach and the hammock or the swamp prickly-pears *(Opuntia)* abounded. There were several kinds—*Opuntia dillenii, O. zebrina, O. abjecta, O. ochrocentra.* There were no signs of hybridization, although the plants of the different species often grew intermixed.

Two vines were so luxuriant that they smothered shrubs just as the woe-vine *(Cassytha)* often does in the scrub.[38] They were a milkweed *(Metastelma blodgettii)* and a grape *(Cissus trifoliata).* The cheese-shrub *(Morinda roioc)* was quite yellow with ripe fruit. This fruit, together with the strong odor of the Jamaica-dogwood, furnished the opposite kind of odor to that of the mosquito-plant referred to above. The madder family was well represented by additional plants—seven-year apple *(Casasia),* box-brier *(Randia),* black-torch *(Erithalis),* snowberry *(Chiococca),* and ernodea *(Ernodea).*

The black-mangrove *(Avicennia)* exhibited an interesting variation of its root-system. It grew both in the swamp and on the dry sand-ridge. In the wet swamps the numerous "quills"—corresponding to the "knees" of the cypress-trees—were present; on the dry ridge the "quills" were not formed, at least they did not rise above the sand so as to be in evidence.

It was dark when we cast anchor off the settlement on the eastern side of Big Pine. The stars appeared in the sky and likewise in the water, the latter lights being caused by hundreds of jelly-fish floating in the water. All these lights soon disappeared when the heavens became overcast, and for twelve hours we had an electric-pyrotechnic display at every point of the compass. When the rain ceased in the morning, we went ashore for a day's exploration, at the same time anticipating a terrible mosquito scourge. However, in this we were pleasantly disappointed.

Our plan was a rapid survey of the hammocks of the island and observations on cacti. Incidentally we sought the long-lost species of fat-pork *(Clusia)* that was found on Big Pine Key in the earlier half of the last century and since sought in vain. In passing, it may be of interest to note that the West Indian plants collected in the same period as was the fat-pork, and since eliminated from the records of our flora by the "Doubting Thomases" have been rediscovered. They are: *Phyllanthus speciousus* and *Cupania glabra.*

The primeval plant-covering of Big Pine Key, which was, doubtless, originally uniform hammock, was ages ago mostly transformed into pineland-palmland. The one-time uniform hammock growth was gradually separated into individual hammocks. Even if the original vegetation comprised uniformly identical species, the different positions and local conditions of the hammocks would soon cause them to become individualized by the natural elimination of species and perhaps the addition of others from distant points. The advent and sojourn of the red men or aborigines in one or more waves doubtless modified these hammocks further. The advent of the white man has not only greatly accelerated the evolution, but has resulted in the absolute destruction of many hammocks within the past and the present generations.

As far as our explorations have progressed, seven hammock or one-time hammock areas have come to our notice: (A) Along the eastern shore north of the "Doctor's Arm," which is the peninsula opposite the northern end of No Name Key. Now, scarcely any growth that might be hammock remains there, but there is an occasional tree or clump of shrubs and trees consisting usually of what appears to have been the peculiarly characteristic woody plant of the former hammock, namely, an endemic varnish-leaf *(Dodonaea microcarya),* not now known elsewhere on the island. (B) Along the shore on the opposite side of the island there are scattered hammocks where the recently rediscovered cupania *(Cupania glabra)* of the soapberry family is abundant. The tree is not known elsewhere this side of the Gulf Stream. A note on these hammocks has been published in a former botanical article.[39] (C) On the eastern side of the key south of the "Doctor's Arm" are a few remnants of a once extensive hammock. There the peculiar shrub and tree is the savia *(Savia bahamensis)* of the spurge family. This plant is not known elsewhere this side of the Gulf Stream.[40] (D) Near the south side of the oölitic part of the key is the hammock where the largest and most numerous trees of the locust-berry *(Byrsonima lucida)* of the malphigia family are known in Florida. (E) On the southwestern point of the oölitic part of the key is a curious hammock comprising a mixture of high hammock and low hammock woody plants. There trees of the Joe-wood *(Jacquinia keyensis)* of the Joe-wood family, with trunks a foot in diameter, and the black-torch *(Erithalis fruticosa)* of the madder family, found for the first time as a tree, with a trunk up to half a foot in diameter, stood out prominently among the other vegetation.

The remaining hammock areas to be mentioned are on the coral limestone part of the key. (F) On the southern front is the hammock described on a preceding page, where the peculiarly branched Jamaica-dogwood *(Ichthyomethia piscipula)* of the pea family is the prominent woody plant. (G) On the southeastern point of the coral limestone formation is the large hammock of typical highland shrubs and trees, together with the wonderful cactus development in which ten different kinds of these remarkable succulents abound.[41] Much more in general and in detail could be written regarding the hammocks and the pinelands of Big Pine Key, but lack of space forbids. However, among the many phenomena of interest, the absence of epiphytic orchids in the hammocks is striking. The widely distributed tree-orchid *(Encyclia tampensis)* is the only one we have noticed, and that in sparing quantities.

Big Pine Key is also celebrated for its zoology. There are

three kinds of mammals on the island, two native—the raccoon and the deer, which has lately been found to represent a species distinct from the common deer of Florida; and one naturalized—the domestic cat has taken to the woods where it maintains itself and is said to have become as wild as the native lynx of the State. The alligator, and perhaps also the crocodile, are rather common in the rock erosion holes. The rattlesnake is the only other large animal inhabiting the island. Animal life, as well as vegetable, has persisted in spite of continuous slaughter.

The deer, for example, has been hunted ever since the advent of the white man in that region, and large numbers, considering the small area and isolated position, have been killed every year for several generations; yet the supply maintains itself. But, this was not the beginning of the killing off of the mammals, for on the western side of the island, at the point we visited on this excursion, there is an aboriginal village site and Indian mound comprising apparently between six and eight acres of hammock land. We are safe in assuming that the old red man drew on the animals of the land as well as those of the sea for his food supply. How fascinating, yet exasperating, it is to speculate as to the origin, the mode of life, the cause and time of the extermination of a settlement that flourished on the site just mentioned!

Aboriginal Ruins on Bay Biscayne

After our return from the Florida Keys, studies on the Indian mounds and their floras were continued.

We visited an aboriginal village site and burial mound in the mangroves near the mouth of Indian Creek in the upper end of Bay Biscayne, then known only to a few residents of the mainland. The village site is a triangular plateau bordering the lagoon.

It is about a quarter of a mile from the ocean beach. The sides are about a hundred yards long. It is elevated above the maximum high water and is built of sand and discarded shells of species that grow both in the ocean and in the bay. Thus it is in part a kitchen-midden. The surrounding vegetation is mangrove and it is encompassed by water at high tide. On it one finds a hammock—a bit of high hammock vegetation right in the mangroves. The burial mound is directly north of the village site. It is about a hundred feet in diameter and higher than the village site. A great many bodies were interred there. By reaching under the loose sand a skull could be located almost anywhere. The bodies were apparently deposited in various positions. Many of them indicated death by violence, as a pierced skull or fractured skull. The superficial burials may represent the period just after the discovery of America, for some of the skulls seem to be other than Indian and would thus represent the remains of shipwrecked Europeans who may have been killed in attacks by the red men, or have died natural deaths while prisoners, or have been the victims of sacrificial ceremonies which were practiced among the aborigines.[42]

In some way the Seminoles knew of this burial mound, although it represents the generation of Indians living there before their advent. A Seminole known as Croppy-head Charley—his ears had been cut off for some real or supposed offense—who died at the reputed age of one hundred and ten years, during the late epidemic of influenza, said that the remains in the mound were the bodies of all the old men of the village who had been killed off by the young men in order to get rid of them. Of course, this probably is one of the myths that gain credence among such people, based on something that excited the imagination. But while this is, apparently, not the source of the burial mound in question, the aborigines often must have been glad to be rid of the old, as the following quotation indicates:

"They mourn all their dead in this manner, old people excepted, to whom they do not pay any attention, saying that these have had their time and are no longer of any use, but only take space and food from the children."[43]

The arboreous vegetation of this aboriginal ruin is quite extensive in spite of the unusual situation. It comprises fully twenty tropical trees, such as two stoppers *(Eugenia),* mastic *(Sideroxylon),* poison-wood *(Metopium),* paradise-tree *(Simaruba glauca),* gumbo-limbo *(Elaphrium),* marlberry *(Icacorea),* sea-grape *(Coccolobis),* pigeon-plum *(Coccolobis),* wild-lime *(Zanthoxylum),* strangling-fig *(Ficus),* seven-year-apple *(Casasia),* coco-plum *(Chrysobalanus).* Some of the shrubs were wild-coffee *(Psychotria),* cankerberry *(Solanum),* skunk-bush *(Petiveria),* snowberry *(Chiococca),* cat-brier *(Smilax),* wild-bamboo *(Lasiacus).* Epiphytes were not wanting: the tree-orchid *(Encyclia tampensis)* and the Boston-fern *(Nephrolepis exaltata)* grew on the rough-barked trees.

The Indians doubtless had their fields on the adjoining sand dunes, where we now find scattered plants of the coontie or conti *(Zamia),* which may represent the descendents of one of the crops they grew, derived originally from the pinelands of the mainland. Their other source of flour—*Smilax*—is also common all over the dunes. The Seminoles inherited these from the aborigines, for we find records of their *Conti-Hateka,* white-flour, referring to the zamia, and the *Conti-Chatee,* red-flour, referring to the smilax. The other common local foods used by them in season were the coco-plum *(Chrysobalanus icaco),* sea-grape *(Coccolobis uvifera),* pigeon-plum *(Coccolobis laurifolia),* gopher-apple *(Geobalanus oblongifolius),* the saw-palmetto *(Serenoa repens),* the cabbage-tree *(Sabal palmetto),* and the prickly-pears *(Opuntiae).*

On the village site above referred to, the strangling-fig *(Ficus aurea)* and the mastic *(Sideroxylon mastichodendron)* grow to gigantic size—a number of the trees are over five feet in diameter. One fig shows three "generations" of growth, i.e., there are two great trunks prostrate, the first almost wholly decayed, and the third erect. In the salt swamp are giant mulberry trees *(Morus),* perhaps descendants of those grown by the aborigines for their fruits and bark. Some of these show two or three vegetative "generations," the fallen trunks have sprouted and made new trees just as is the case of the figs above referred to. The peculiar herb in the salt swamp near the mulberry trees is a kind of native "honeysuckle" *(Diapedium)* which grows as high as one's head and bears leaves a foot long.

This prehistoric relic and its vegetation has been referred to at some length not only because it is an interesting subject, but in order to put it on permanent record, for without any doubt within a few years both the ruins and its vegetation will be wiped off the map and sold as building lots by speculators in land.[44]

Mounds and Floristics of Cape Sable

The jungle of Cape Sable attracted us again, and we devoted two days to further studies there. We drove directly to the settlement of Flamingo and thence westward over the prairies to the rear of Northwest Cape or the southern end of the Ten Thousand Islands, or in latitude only about forty miles south of where we had lately been at Cape Romano, but with the Ten Thousand Islands filling the gap. The mere idea of such motor-car travel in that part of Florida a few years ago would have been thought fantastic. Today it is a reality.

The great prairies west of Flamingo are bordered by hammocks towards the bay. The hammocks are usually fringed by the Spanish-bayonet *(Yucca aloifolia),* often growing in impenetrable thickets without the admixture of other woody plants. The wild cotton also covers acres of prairie land and it is continuously in flower and in fruit the year round. Back of East

Cape Sable the hammocks are also fringed with armed plants, but in this case of different kinds of cacti, prickly-pears, principally *Opuntia dillenii* and dildoe *(Acanthocereus floridanus).* Out that way, too, there are numerous oases of clumps of cabbage-trees *(Sabal)* and of thatch-palm *(Thrinax).* Beyond East Cape we ran to the eastern shore of Whitewater Lake which parallels the shore for many miles. We drove parallel with it to its upper end. There the prairies were carpeted with great patches of various shades of green—the gray-green of the sea-oxeye *(Borrichia frutescens),* yellow-green of the saltwort *(Batis maritima),* deep-green of the sea-purslane *(Sesuvium portulacastrum),* light-green of the samphire *(Salicornia ambigua),* and red of the sea-blite *(Dondia maritima).* Most of these plants were dwarf and rarely exceeded a foot in height. Between Middle Cape and Northwest Cape we ran through miles of switch-grass *(Spartina)* placed so thick that for hundreds of yards the ground was not visible. There curious hammocks appeared towards the Gulf shore. The dominant tree in them was the soapberry *(Sapindus saponaria).* Associated with it were both kinds of caper-trees *(Capparis)* and wild-coffee *(Colubrina colubrina),* and two spinescent trees—wild-lime *(Zanthoxylum fagara)* and box-brier *(Randia aculeata),* the latter again a true tree, as we had found it along the Halpatioke River[45] and on Big Pine Key, as already recorded. The trunks of all the trees in these hammocks were covered with lichens of various genera. Further on there were also hammocks of stopper *(Eugenia)* and of saffron-plum *(Bumelia).* These two kinds of hammocks could be distinguished at long range, for the stopper has erect, often strictly erect branches, while the saffron-plum has widely spreading branches.

Back of Middle Cape we ran over a Liliputian forest of several acres in extent, composed of miniature trees of the box-brier *(Randia),* mostly less than one foot tall. The plants were in flower and in fruit. The flowers were abundant enough to render the air decidedly fragrant thereabouts.

On some of the higher prairies there were thickets of

armed plants only—those mentioned above, prickly-pear, dildoe, and Spanish-bayonet! The stems of the latter were often clothed with the drooping dead leaves after the manner of the Washington palm *(Neowashingtonia robusta).* Curiously enough, the saw-palmetto *(Serenoa repens)* was wanting in all this variety of plant covering. It reappears on the lower Florida Keys fifty miles distant over the Bay of Florida.

Vast white-mangrove *(Laguncularia)* swamps flank the Cape Sable prairies on the north. The growth is particularly luxuriant and the trees give off aerial roots after the manner of the red-mangrove *(Rhizophora mangle).*

We returned to the main canal and followed the embankment westward for several miles to the vicinity of Gator Lake, paralleling our course on the prairie, but several miles to the north of it. Little of interest was disclosed, except the vast mangrove swamp and the epiphytic plants growing on tree-trunks. The luxuriant growth of epiphytes in this vicinity is phenomenal. There are twelve kinds of orchids, some of almost gigantic size, and eleven kinds of bromeliads. In addition, the prickly-pears *(Opuntiae)* and prickly-apples *(Harrisia)* are commonly epiphytic. However, near the aboriginal canal referred to on an earlier page, there is much of interest, thanks to the activities of a former race of red men. Isolated in the vast mangrove swamp there are three Indian mounds comprised of marl. The smaller mounds are roundish, the larger one is oblong, about one hundred feet wide and a hundred yards long. It lies in a southeasterly and northwesterly direction. Just below the mounds is a colony of saw-cabbage palm *(Paurotis wrightii)* with tall and remarkable slender stems. Palms and savages were frequent associates; not only did the Indians use them for the food and the raiment they furnished, but with this type of plant they also sought to satisfy certain vague cravings of the soul, just as palms are used in certain ecclesiastical practices today. We are not surprised, therefore, to find the royal-palm *(Roystonea regia)* there also. About two dozen trees stand on and about the mounds. These and scattered specimens along or near the banks of the old canal are doubtless the descendants of the plants grown there by the primitive red man who built and used the mounds.

These mounds lay directly in the path of the Ingraham Highway running from Miami to Cape Sable. With commendable but almost unheard of forethought the land company which owns the site, had the highway and accompanying canal made in a semicircle around one side of the mounds, instead of cutting directly though and destroying them.

One of several questions that arise in connection with these mounds and also those on Bay Biscayne, is: why were they made in the midst of mangrove swamps? Perhaps they were not thus situated when they were made. They may have been on high open ground or in high hammock. It is generally admitted that the Atlantic Coastal Plain is gradually sinking. Now, in dredging the present canal close to the mounds, skeletons were found lower down than the minimum water-table. The aborigines would hardly have buried their dead below the water-table. The question then rises: has the land been gradually sinking since the burials in question took place? A few feet of former elevation would have maintained an open prairie or high hammock growth instead of the present mangrove swamp!

The vegetation on the mounds shows great variety compared with that of the surrounding mangrove swamps. The more abundant trees were pigeon-plum *(Coccolobis laurifolia),* wild-tamarind *(Lysiloma bahamensis),* guiana-plum *(Drypetes lateriflora),* gumbo-limbo *(Elaphrium simaruba),* manchineel *(Hippomane mancinella),* butterbough *(Exothea paniculata),* coral-bean *(Erythrina arborea),* wild-cinnamon *(Canella winteriana),* mastic *(Sideroxylon mastichodendron),* Jamaica-dogwood *(Ichthyomethia piscipula).* In addition to the royal-palms there were tall specimens of the cabbage-tree *(Sabal palmetto).* Epiphytes were abundant, especially around the base of the mound. Several genera, including the smaller kinds of orchids, such as *Encyclia, Anacheilium, Amphiglottis, Spathiger, Epicladium,* and *Polystachya* were observed. The larger tree-orchids were much in evidence on account of the big plants of *Onicidium,* both *Oncidium undulatum* and *Oncidium floridanum,* with showy flower-panicles on stalks four to eight feet long. Bromeliads were represented by four genera, long-moss *(Dendropogon),* wild-pines *(Tillandsia and Catopsis),* and by our only species of *Guzmannia,* a plant with clusters of narrow green leaves, which grew in great masses over the low woody vegetation. Each plant sends up a flower-stalk a foot to eighteen inches tall, which is cloaked with broad bracts. The bracts at the upper end subtending the flowers are scarlet. As the fruits develop the bracts now lower down as the flower-stalk grows, turn green and are striped dark and light green. Plants with variegated leaves are occasionally seen.

The wild cotton *(Gossypium punctatum)* is plentiful in the vicinity of the mounds. North of the Florida Keys, where it is widespread, cotton is often found only at and near the former settlements of the red man. He doubtless used it and perhaps cultivated it to some extent. The use of another fiber the white man inherited from the red man is that of the leaves of the Spanish bayonet *(Yucca aloifolia)*—for string.

Observations Along the Eastern Coast

On our homeward course we skirted the eastern coast as far as the mouth of the Saint John's River, mainly for studies in prickly-pears. Little attention was paid to other groups of plants, but some observations made *en route* may be of general interest.

The sandy bluffs of Saint Lucie Sound backed by the tropical hammock of shrubs, trees, and woody vines were clothed with herbaceous vines. Curiously enough, of the ten kinds of vines observed in passing, five were naturalized exotics and five were natives. The natives were cat-brier *(Smilax beyrichii),* gray-nicker *(Guilandina crista),* coin-vine *(Dalbergia ecastophyllum),* grape *(Vitis cinerea?),* and wild muscadine *(Muscadinia munsoniana).* The naturalized vines were: poke-vine *(Agdestis clematidea),* Barbados-gooseberry *(Pereskia pereskia),* two thunbergias *(Thunbergia alta, T. fragrans),* and a balsam-apple *(Momordica balsamea).* The climate is peculiarly tempered there, for the mango and other tender tropical trees are hardy as well as the trees of the native tropical hammock. This Fort Pierce hammock is repeated, in part at least, forty miles further north in latitude, at the mouth of the Sebastian River. This and various former aboriginal settlements along the eastern coast have been designated for future exploration.

Local rains had caused vegetation to advance in some places more than in others. Back of the Cape Canaveral region there were many flowering plants in the woods, both among the pines and in the hammocks. The tar-flower *(Befaria racemosa)* had raised up its panicles of white or pinkish stars above the accompanying scrubby vegetation. It occurs in the pinelands just as its relative, the Chapman-honeysuckle *(Rhododendron chapmanii)* does in the Saint Joseph's Bay region in western Florida. In the high hammocks the iron-weed *(Vernonia altissima)* grew both scattered and massed. The brilliant purple of the numerous heads was the most conspicuous object in the landscape. The low hammocks were naturally the more floriferous localities. White prevailed among the flowers—milkweed *(Asclepias perennans),* man-of-the-earth *(Ipomoea pandurata),* chaff-acanthus *(Tubiflora angustifolia),* and spider-lilies *(Hymenocallis).* Color was not wanting, however, for in the morning, as it was, the rose-pink ruellia *(Ruellia parviflora)* was at its best, and blue lobelias grew copiously in the wet depressions. There was an unusually copious growth of the great bulrush

(Scirpus validus) in the marshes. The plants were often nearly ten feet tall and resembled almost perfectly the carriage whip so common a generation ago.

In passing through the Halifax River region we revisited the kitchen-midden referred to on a preceding page as Green Mound. This is one of the higher shell-mounds and commands a fine view over the coastal dunes in all directions and the mainland to the westward. Its plant covering is largely tropical, as is that of the neighboring mounds. On its summit we added another tropical plant not only to the list of the flora of these middens, but also to that of the North American mainland—a heliotrope-vine *(Tournefortia poliochros).* The north and the south often meet on these mounds. In this case the tropical vine just mentioned was intertwined with the more typically northern Virginia-creeper *(Parthenocissus quinquefolia).* The live-oaks on this mound seem to grow in even more fantastic shapes than they do on any of the neighboring mounds. Massive trees do not send their trunks, often one or two feet in diameter, erect as columnar shafts, but spread them horizontally on or near the ground in serpentine or cork-screw-like fashion.[46] The trunks and similarly contorted branches resemble great writhing saurians.

Alas, since writing the above reference to Green Mound, this kitchen-midden also has been shorn of its natural native growth, and exotic weeds have promptly taken possession of the whole surface, this repeating the process met with throughout the State.

Now to recapitulate concerning the wholesale destruction of Florida's unique monuments of Nature. Florida has passed through several cycles of configuration. It was alternately raised above the sea and submerged several times. With each more recent cycle the surface was sculptured by the elements and populated by plants and animals. What the early configuration of the land and constituents of the flora were we cannot even imagine with any degree of accuracy. Natural changes, both constructive and destructive, continued to modify the landscape and its makeup after the advent of primeval man. Early man, without doubt, augmented the negative methods and processes of Nature, by introducing some destructive agencies of his own. Facts about this period, although relatively recent, are completely unknown and will remain so. It was not until the Florida aborigines appeared on the scene and later gave the Spanish expeditioners a generous course of hard luck that we get the first documentary evidence of human vandalism. For the sake of emphasis we shall quote again an early record by Alvar Nuñez Cabeza de Vaca:

Prophecies

"Those from further inland have another remedy, just as bad and even worse, which is to go about with a firebrand, setting fire to the plains and timber so as to drive off the mosquitoes, and also to get lizards and similar things which they eat to come out of the soil. In the same manner they kill deer, encircling them with fires, and they do it also to deprive the animals of pasture, compelling them to go for food where the Indians went. For never they build abodes except where there are wood and water, and sometimes load themselves with the requisites and go in quest of deer, which are found mostly where there is neither water nor wood."

Several centuries later William Barton, on a journey to Florida observed about conditions on the borderland:

"There is, as yet, but little naked sandy desert; but should the weather continue, a few years longer, as dry as it has been for the last two years—and fires should rage as extensively destroying the vegetation—a large portion of the maritime part of Georgia on the frontiers of Florida would be rendered like the deserts of Arabia. Were I a member of the Georgia Legislature, my most strenuous exertions would be made to prevent, by law the burning of the Forests, —which impoverishes the land, and does incalculable mischief, without one single advantage resulting from it. Yet many of the stupid people do it, to destroy the rattle-snake—make the grass grow—and I believe for the fun of looking at it."

From the period just referred to the forces of destruction have gathered until today their action is fast and furious, and the results superlative. It is true that constant change involving destruction is a natural process as well as an artificial one. However, Nature's method is relatively slow and, as a rule, orderly, and results are usually finished—constructive—and satisfactory, while man's methods are crude and rapid, and result in great disorder. This is indicative of Florida's tomorrow. Yesterday a botanical paradise! Tomorrow, the desert!

Florida's devastation is dreaded by John Gifford in his book "Billy Bowlegs." "Although there are no mountains of sand and rock, there are mountains of clouds; instead of desert sands there are green glades and prairies dotted with glistening lakes and water courses; here and there in the broad expanse are islands of cypress or pine; the cranes, herons and other birds are everywhere, but the picture will lose a vital part when the Seminole with his little family in his dug-out canoe quits it forever. Florida is not all mud and sand, She has broad, dry treeless prairies and miles of pine covered and lake dotted sand hills; a feast for the eyes of any globe trotter, and rocky bluffs on the ocean shore besides its miles of muddy glades and moss-decked swamps. And there too hid away in the swamps of the south are two or three patches of royal palm, the most majestic of trees, passing on like the Seminole into the realm of the past, and there too is the mahogany, the prince of all hardwoods, destined like the flamingo, the parakeet and ibis and many other choice products of nature to pass on with the Seminole. All these and lots of other things that formed the Florida of yesterday must no doubt in time fall before the juggernaut of modern progress. We try hard to preserve the old furniture that our ancestors sat and slept in, but neglect the things that can never be replaced or even imitated.

"When the trees are all turpentined and cut, when even the moss of the trees has all been gathered and sold for the stuffing of cushions and mattresses, when the cattle are tick-infested and of little value, and fires have reduced the land to a useless scrub, and when the agricultural crop consists mainly of cane to produce syrup for the manufacture of liquor, white, negro and Indian are all on the same plane. They easily revert to a very primitive state, all freely mingle, all 'tote' guns and are all naturally vindictive toward anything that stands in their way. The white is of course the worst. He falls hardest because he falls farthest."

Here is a unique El Dorado, mainly a tongue of land, extending hundreds of miles into tepid waters, reaching, almost to the Tropic of Cancer, where the floristics of temperate, subtropic, and tropic regions not only meet, but mingle; where the animals of temperate regions associate with those of the tropics. As much as possible of this natural history museum should be preserved, not only for its beauty, but also for its educational value, for it is within easy reach of the majority of the population of the United States.

Many localities whose natural features, now destroyed, are not duplicated elsewhere, could easily have been made state or federal reservations, if the public officials had had the proper interest and foresight in such matters. In Florida, aside from Royal Palm State Park and Turtle Mound, there are no reservations for the preservation of the natural features, except those maintained by a few interested individuals, and a partly developed national forest. Steps for protection of selected areas should be taken at once by the state and federal governments. It is not yet too late to act.

Photo by John Kunkel Small/Florida State Archives

The top of a kitchen-midden—Castle Mound—on the dunes opposite Port Orange, Florida. This aboriginal monument, as left by the aborigines, was between twenty-five and thirty feet high. The crown of rock represents the top of the core where a fire, either for a beacon or for cooking, burned the shells into quick-lime as the mound increased in height. On slaking, the shell material solidified. When the kitchen-midden was removed for building county roads this core was the last part to be reduced.

Photo by John Kunkel Small/Florida State Archives

The spot where the shell-mound stood, a year after the above picture on the accompanying plate was made. The kitchen-midden has been removed. The sand foundation is shown with scattered oyster shells on the surface. The oyster-bars where the Indians gathered the oysters are still extant and extensively exposed at low tide in the adjacent lagoon. The vegetation of such mounds is largely tropical shrubs. With the reduction of the mound a plant association unique in the region disappears.

A hammock island in the Everglades in the southern part of Dade County, Florida, with a single royal-palm in the center. These hammocks comprise an association of warm-temperate and tropical trees which act as hosts for various flowering air-plants—wild-pines and orchids, including three kinds of vanilla. They served as an ideal refuge for reptiles, birds, and mammals.

Photo by John Kunkel Small/Florida State Archives

Photo by John Kunkel Small/Florida State Archives

A view showing the result of vandalism. A hammock in the same region as that in the next preceding plate, which has been also ravished since the picture was taken, burning at night. Not only hundreds, but thousands of such hammocks throughout the southern half of the Everglades have been burned during the past decade. Some have been utterly destroyed, not a vestige of the vegetation remaining.

Photo by John Kunkel Small/Florida State Archives

In Royal Palm State Park, Dade County, Florida. A bed of wood-fern on the jungle floor. The two more conspicuous elements in the floristics of the hammock were the heads of the royal-palms raised high above the hammock roof and the marvelous beds of ferns on the floor. There were eighteen kinds of ferns within the hammock—about a dozen terrestrial and half a dozen epiphytic. The leaves of the terrestrial ones varied greatly in size —from a quarter of an inch to over twenty-seven feet long.

Photo by John Kunkel Small/Florida State Archives

The same spot as above after being fire-swept, with even the humus floor-covering burned down to the rock foundation. In the back-ground may be seen three royal-palms over one hundred and thirty feet tall, some of the survivors of the original one hundred and eight palms. In the middle-ground stand the skeletons of various hard-wood trees, the large live-oak on the right having once supported an extensive hanging garden of air-plants. In the fore-ground lie the charred remains of a giant live-oak, which tree with its similar associates once formed the second conspicuous arboreous element in the hammock.

Crocodile Hole, a small bay in the mangroves along Indian Creek opposite Miami, Florida. Here the crocodile was first found in North America just before the last quarter of the nineteenth century. The alligator was definitely known in Florida almost from the time of the discovery of America. The mangrove trees, with the exception of a few air-plants on their stems and some aquatic plants about their roots, usurped the shores, forming a canopy of exceptional beauty.

Photo by John Kunkel Small/Florida State Archives

Photo by John Kunkel Small/Florida State Archives

The same spot as shown in the accompanying plate. The last vestige of the plant life here was destroyed in changing this place from a reptilian to mammalian place to abode. On the sandy dunes adjacent to the mangroves now buried under a layer of marl and sand, formerly grew rare and showy plants, among which rose-purple flowers were a conspicuous feature; for example a candy-root each of whose flowers showed a central speck of gold and a four-o'clock relative with large infertile flowers and small inconspicuous flowers which burrowed and produced fruits under the ground.

Photos by John Kunkel Small/Florida State Archives

The top of a burial mound on an aboriginal site in the mangrove swamp on the eastern side of Bay Biscayne, Florida. The sand was carried into the mangroves from the coastal dunes. Upon this settlement area raised above the tides a hammock of berry-bearing trees sprung up. The seeds of the original trees were brought there either by the Indians or by birds and mammals. The soil, enriched by the mode of life of the aborigines, supported a luxuriant hammock. Its vigor was evident after several centuries of disuse.

Photo by John Kunkel Small/Florida State Archives

The same mound a year after the accompanying picture was made, wrecked as a result of real estate developments. Only a few plant skeletons now stand above the numerous human skeletons in the sand of the mound. The "subdivision," had it survived, whose promoters are responsible for the wreckage here shown, might just as well have included a beautiful city park, already developed, planted by the aborigines centuries ago. This Indian settlement comprised a large triangular village site proper and the burial mound.

Glossary

This glossary provides a cross-reference for scientific names referenced by Small to names used in the current *Flora of Florida* by Wunderlin and Hansen (2003). Where possible, the common name used by Small within this document, the updated scientific name with published authority, status as a listed species, where applicable, and other pertinent information, where applicable, are included for each scientific name used by Small. Content was derived primarily from the bibliography listed below and from the author's experience. Any omissions or errors in applying scientific names to species within this document are the author's responsibility. Abbreviations: FDACS - Florida Department of Agriculture and Consumer Services, USFWS - U.S. Fish and Wildlife Service, WH - Wunderlin and Hansen 2003.

Acanthocereus floridanus
"dildoe"; *Acanthocereus tetragonus* (L.) Hummelinck; listed as threatened by FDACS

Agdestis clematidea
"poke-vine"; *Agdestis clematidea* Moç. & Sessé ex DC.; listed as non-native by WH and Small

Agave decipiens
"century-plant"; *Agave decipiens* Baker - false sisal

Agave neglecta
"Florida century plant"; *Agave neglecta* Small; its location in the "Tomoka region" (the Daytona/New Smyrna region) would represent an extension to the known range of this species to Volusia County and/or Brevard County on the east coast of Florida

Agave rigida
"sisal"; likely *Agave sisalana* Perrine - sisal hemp, listed as an non-native by WH, but not noted as non-native by Small

Aletris
"colic-root"; likely *Aletris bracteata* Northr. - which is listed as endangered by FDACS, although it could possibly be *Aletris lutea* Small as well

Ambrosia artemisiifolia
"ragweed"; *Ambrosia artemisiifolia* L.

Amphiglottis
the generic synonym for several species of *Epidendrum;* species undetermined

Amphiglottis conopsia
"temperate tree-orchid"; commonly referred to as *Epidendrum conopseum* R. Br., but recently an earlier name *E. magnoliae* Muhl was found to predate this commonly used scientific name and, thus, would be more appropriate by the rules of taxonomy.

Amygdalus
"peach"; Prunus persica (L.) Batsch - common peach; listed as non-native by WH and Small

Amygdalus persica
"peach"; *Prunus persica* (L.) Batsch - common peach; listed as non-native by WH and Small

alligator
Alligator mississippiensis

Anacheilium
likely *Prosthechea cochleata* (L.) W.E. Higgins, which is listed as endangered by FDACS

Anamomis longipes
Species Undetermined

Anamomis simpsonii
"spice-tree"; *Myrcianthes fragrans* (Sw.) McVaugh - Simpson's stopper; listed as threatened by FDACS

Apple
likely *Malus* sp.

Asclepias lanceolata
"milkweed"; *Asclepias lanceolata* Walter

Asclepias perennans
"milkweed"; *Asclepias perennis* Walter

Ascyrum
"St. Peter's-wort"; likely *Hypericum crux-andreae* (L.) Crantz

Asimina
"dwarf pawpaw"; likely *Asimina pygmea* (W. Bartram) Dunal, although other "dwarf" *Asimina* spp. occur within the traveled areas

Atamosco
"atamas-lily"; likely *Zephyranthes atamasca* (L.) Herb. var. *treatiae* (S. Watson) Meerow - Treat's zephyrlily; listed as threatened by FDACS

Atamosco simpsonii
"pine-lily"; *Zephyranthes simpsonii* Chapm. - redmargin zephylily, Simpson's rain lily; listed as threatened by FDACS

Avicennia
"black mangrove"; *Avicennia germinans* (L.) L.

Baccharis
"groundsel bush"; *Baccharis halimifolia* L.

Baptisia alba
"false-indigo"; *Baptisia alba* (L.) Vent. - white wild indigo

Batis maritima
"saltwort"; *Batis maritima* L.

Befaria racemosa
"tarflower"; *Bejaria racemosa* Vent.

Berlandiera humilis
"green-eye"; *Berlandiera pumila* (Michx.) Nutt.

Bidens leucantha
"beggar's-ticks"; *Bidens alba* (L.) DC.

Blackberry bushes
Rubus spp.

Bladderwort
Utricularia spp. - Species undetermined

Blechnum serrulatum
"swamp-bracken"; *Blechnum serrulatum* Rich. - swamp fern

Blue-stem
Sabal minor (Jacq.) Pers.

Boehmeria cylindrica
"false-nettle"; *Boehmeria cylindrica* (L.) Sw.

Boerhaavia coccinea
"Dr. Garber's potato"; *Boerhavia diffusa* L.

Borrichia frutescens
"sea-oxeye"; *Borrichia frutescens* (L.) DC.

Bradleya frutescens
"swamp wisteria"; likely *Wisteria frutescens* (L.) Poir. - American wisteria

Brassia caudata
"spider-orchid"; *Brassia caudata* (L.) Lindl.; listed as endangered by FDACS; has not been seen in Florida since the late 1960's despite repeated searches.

Buchnera
"blue-hearts"; *Buchnera americana* L.

Bumelia
"saffron-plum"; *Sideroxylon celastrinum* (Kunth) T.D. Penn.

Bumelia angustifolia
"saffron-plum"; *Sideroxylon celastrinum* (Kunth) T.D. Penn.

Bumelia tenax
"gum-elastic"; *Sideroxylon tenax* L. - tough bully

Byrsonima lucida
"spring-locust-berry"; *Byrsonima lucida* (Mill.) DC.

Cabbage
Brassica oleracea L.

Cakile lanceolata
"sea-rocket"; *Cakile lanceolata* (Willd.) O.E. Schultz

Callitriche nuttallii
"water-starwort"; *Callitriche pedunculosa* Nutt.; listed as non-native by WH

Calyptranthes zuzygium
"myrtle-of-the-river"; *Calyptranthes zuzygium* (L.) Sw.; listed as endangered by FDACS

Canella winteriana
"wild-cinnamon"; *Canella winterana* (L.) Gaertn.; listed as endangered by FDACS

Capparis
"both kinds of caper-tree"; *Capparis cynophallophora* L. and C. flexuosa (L.) L.

Capriola dactylon
"Bermuda-grass"; *Cynodon dactylon* (L.) Pers.; listed as non-native by WH

Capsicum baccatum
"bird-pepper"; *Capsicum annuum* L.

Carex
"sedges"; *Carex* spp.

Carica papaya
"papaya"; *Carica papaya* L.; shown as an non-native by WH, but not noted as non-native by Small

Casasia
"seven-year apple"; *Genipa clusiifolia* (Jacq.) Griseb.

cassena *(Ilex)*
"cassena" or "cassina" was historically used as a common name for two *Ilex* species: *Ilex vomitoria* Aiton - yaupon holly and *Ilex cassine* L. - dahoon holly. In the dunes, Small is likely referring to yaupon holly.

Cassytha
"woe-vine"; *Cassytha filiformis* L. - love vine

Castalia
"water-lily"; possibly *Nymphaea odorata* Sol. or, less likely, *Nymphaea mexicana* Zucc.

Casuarina
"Australian-pine"; likely *Casuarina equisetifolia* L.

Cathartolinum
"yellow-flax"; *Linum* sp.

Catopsis
"wild-pine"; *Catopsis* spp. - Species undetermined.

Celery
Apium graveolens L.

Celtis mississippiensis
"sugar-berry"; *Celtis laevigata* Willd.

Centunculus pentandrus
"chaffweed"; *Anagallis pumila* Sw. - Florida pimpernel

Cerothamnus
"wax-myrtle"; likely *Myrica cerifera* L.

Cerothamnus ceriferus
"bayberry", "wax-myrtle"; *Myrica cerifera* L.

Chamaecrista brachiata
"big partridge-pea"; *Chamaecrista fasciculata* (Michx.) Greene

Chamaelirium
"devil's-bit"; *Chamaelirium luteum* (L.) A. Gray - fairywand

Chamaesyce
"slender spurge"; *Chamaesyce* spp.; Species undetermined.

Chapmannia floridana
Chapmannia floridana Torr. & A. Gray

Chenopodium album
"goosefoot"; *Chenopodium album* L.

Chenopodium ambrosioides
"wormwood"; *Chenopodium ambrosioides* L. - Mexican tea; listed as non-native by WH

Chiococca
"snowberry"; *Chiococca alba* (L.) Hitchc.

Chiococca alba
"snowberry"; *Chiococca alba* (L.) Hitchc.

Chloris Gayana
"Rhodes-grass"; *Chloris gayana* Kunth; listed as non-native by WH

Chrosperma
"fly-poison"; *Amianthium muscaetoxicum* (Walter) A. Gray

Chrysobalanus
"coco-plum"; *Chrysobalanus icaco* L.

Chrysobalanus icaco
"coco-plum"; *Chrysobalanus icaco* L.

Chrysobalanus pellocarpus
"coco-plum"; *Chrysobalanus icaco* L.

Cirsium smallii
"pine-thistle"; *Cirsium horridulum* Michx.

Cissus trifoliate
"grape"; *Cissus trifoliata* (L.) L.

Citrus spinosissima
"lime"; *Citrus xaurantiifolia* (Christm.) Swingle - key lime; listed as non-native by WH

clam
referred to as "Venus" by Small - possibly *Mercenaria mercenaria* L.

Clinopodium coccineum
"showy basil"; *Calamintha coccinea* (Nutt. ex Hook.) Benth.

Clinopodium glabrum
Undetermined. This name is a synonym of *Clinopodium arkansanum* (Nutt.) House, a species not known to occur within Florida (closest known distribution is in Tennessee).

Clusia
"fat-pork"; *Clusia rosea* Jacq.; now known from Dade County and the Keys

Cnidoscolus
"tread-softly"; *Cnidoscolus stimulosus* (Michx.) Engelm. & A. Gray

Coccolobis
with common name "seagrape", then *Coccoloba uvifera* (L.) L.; with common name "pigeon-plum", then *C. diversifolia* Jacq.

Coccolobis laurifolia
"pigeon-plum"; *Coccoloba diversifolia* Jacq.

Coccolobis uvifera
"seagrape"; *Coccoloba uvifera* (L.) L.

Cocos nucifera
"coconut"; *Cocos nucifera* L.; listed as non-native by WH and suggested as planted by Small

Colocasia antiquorum
"dasheen"; *Colocasia esculenta* (L.) Schott - wild taro; listed as non-native by WH and Small

Colubrina colubrina
"wild-coffee"; *Colubrina arborescens* (Mill.) Sarg.; listed as endangered by FDACS

Commelina angustifolia
"dew-flower"; *Commelina erecta* L.

Conoclinium
"mist-flower"; *Conoclinium coelestinum* (L.) DC

conch
likely *Strombus gigas* L. - queen conch

Conti-Chatee
Seminole name for red-four derived from a *Smilax* spp.

Conti-Hateka
Seminole name for white flour derived from coontie (*Zamia pumila* L.)

Coreopsis
"beggar's ticks"; likely *Coreopsis leavenworthii* Torr. & A. Gray

Coreopsis lanceolata
"tickseed"; *Coreopsis lanceolata* L.; listed as non-native by Small - but as a native by WH

Coreopsis leavenworthii
"beggar's ticks"; *Coreopsis leavenworthii* Torr. & A. Gray

Couroupita guianensis
"cannonball-tree"; *Couroupita guianensis* Aubl.; not currently known from the flora of Florida according to WH, the specimen described by Small was likely an introduction

Crocanthemum
"rock roses"; likely *Helianthemum* spp.

crocodile
Crocodylus acutus

Cupania glabra
Cupania glabra Sw. - American toadwood; listed as endangered by FDACS and only found on the Keys within Florida

Cuthbertia
"delicate spiderwort"; likely either *Callisia graminea* (Small) G.C. Tucker - grassleaf roseling or *Callisia ornata* (Small) G.C. Tucker - Florida scrub roseling; both of which were originally described by Small

Cynoxylon
"dogwood"; likely *Cornus florida* L., flowering dogwood

Dalbergia ecastophyllum
"woody coin-vine"; *Dalbergia ecastaphyllum* (L.) Taub.

Datura stramonium
"Jamestown-weed", "Jimson-weed"; *Datura stramonium* L.

Daucus pusillus
"wild carrot"; *Daucus pusillus* Michx.

Dendropogon
"long-moss"; *Tillandsia usneoides* (L.) L. - Spanish moss

deer, a species distinct from the common deer
Odocoileus virginianus clavium - Key deer; listed as endangered by the FFWCC and USFWS; known only from the Keys

Diapedium
"honeysuckle"; likely *Dicliptera sexangularis* (L.) Juss. - sixangle foldwing

Dichromena latifolia
"white-top"; *Rhynchospora latifolia* (Baldwin) W.W. Thomas

Diospyros virginiana
"persimmon"; *Diospyros virginiana* L.

Dipholis salicifolia
"bustic", "cassada"; *Sideroxylon salicifolium* (L.) Lam.

***Dodonaea*, two other species of**
Small notes two other species of *Dodonaea* in Florida. The Big Pine Key endemic is likely *Dodonaea elaeagnoides* Rudolphi ex Ledeb. & Alderstam. The second species found "in the West Indies" is undetermined.

Dodonaea microcarya
"varnish-leaf"; *Dodonaea elaeagnoides* Rudolphi ex Ledeb. & Alderstam; listed as endangered by FDACS and known in the USA only within the Florida Keys - also occurs within several Caribbean islands

Dodonaea viscosa
"varnish-leaf"; *Dodonaea viscosa* Jacq.; is now known from much of the coastal counties of the peninsula

Doellingeria
"false-aster"; likely *Doellingeria sericocarpoides* Small - southern whitetop; named by J.K. Small

Dondia maritima
"sea-blite"; this species name is a synonym with *Suaeda maritima* (L.) Dumort, which occurs generally in the northeastern portion of the U.S. and is not currently known from Florida. This may refer to the Florida species of seep-weed *Suaeda linearis* (Elliott) Moq.

Dracocephalum
"obedient-plant"; likely *Physostegia purpurea* (Walter) S.F. Blake

Drypetes lateriflora
"guiana-plum"; *Drypetes lateriflora* (Sw.) Krug & Urb.; listed as threatened by FDACS

Dwarf-palmetto
Sabal minor (Jacq.) Pers.

Dyschoriste
"calophanes"; likely *Dyschoriste oblongifolia* (Michx.) Kuntze - twinflower

Elaphrium
"gumbo-limbo"; *Bursera simaruba* (L.) Sarg.

Elaphrium Simaruba
"gumbo-limbo"; *Bursera simaruba* (L.) Sarg.

Elm
Ulmus spp.

Encyclia
likely *Encyclia tampensis* (Lindl.) Small; current name originated by Small

Encyclia tampensis
"tropical tree-orchid"; *Encyclia tampensis* (Lindl.) Small; current name originated by Small

Epicladium
refers to *Prosthechea boothiana* var. *erythronioides* (Small) W.E. Higgins; listed as endangered by FDACS; varietal name originated by Small

Erechtites
"fire-weed"; *Erechtites hieraciifolius* (L.) Raf. Ex DC.

Erechtites hieracifolia
"fire-weed"; *Erechtites hieraciifolius* (L.) Raf. Ex DC.

Erianthes
"plume-grass"; likely *Saccharum giganteum* (Walter) Pers.

Eriogonum
"umbrella-plant"; likely *Eriogonum tomentosum* Michx. - wild buckwheat

Eriogonum floridanum
Eriogonum longifolium Nutt. var. *gnaphalifolium* Gand. - scrub buckwheat; listed as endangered by FDACS and threatened by the USFWS

Erithalis
"black-torch"; *Erithalis fruticosa* L.; listed as threatened by FDACS

Erithalis fruticosa
"black-torch"; *Erithalis fruticosa* L.; listed as threatened by FDACS

Ernodea
"ernodea"; likely *Ernodea cokeri* Britton ex Coker; listed as endangered by FDACS

Erythrina arborea
"coral-bean"; *Erythrina herbacea* L.

Eugenia
"stopper"; likely *Eugenia axillaris* (Sw.) Willd. - white stopper for much of the document, but in Bay Biscayne area could be one of several undetermined species of *Eugenia.*

Eugenia axillaris
"stopper"; *Eugenia axillaris* (Sw.) Willd. - white stopper

Eupatorium
"dog-fennel"; likely *Eupatorium capillifolium* (Lam.) Small ex Porter & Britton

Eupatorium capillifolium
"dog-fennel"; *Eupatorium capillifolium* (Lam.) Small ex Porter & Britton; current name originated by Small

Eustachys glauca
"finger-grass"; *Eustachys glauca* Chapm.

Exothea paniculata
"butterbough"; *Exothea paniculata* (Juss.) Radlk. ex T. Durand

Ficus
"strangling-fig"; likely *Ficus aurea* Nutt.

Ficus aurea
"strangling-fig"; *Ficus aurea* Nutt.

Ficus carica
"fig"; *Ficus carica* L.; listed as non-native by WH and Small

Flags
likely *Iris* spp.

Flaveria
"dye-plant"; likely *Flaveria linearis* Lag. - narrowleaf yellowtops or *F. trinervia* (Spreng.) C. Mohr - clustered yellow-tops

Florida-rosemary
Ceratiola ericoides Michx.

Fraxinus lanceolata
"ash"; *Fraxinus pennsylvanica* Marshall

Fothergilla
"witch-alder"; likely *Fothergilla gardenii* L. - dwarf witchalder

Fraxinus
"pop-ash"; *Fraxinus caroliniana* Mill.

Fringe-tree
likely *Chionanthus virginicus* L. - white fringetree, old-man's beard

Froelichia floridana
Froelichia floridana (Nutt.) Moq. - cottonweed

Gaillardia drummondii
"blanket-weed"; *Gaillardia pulchella* Foug. - firewheel; listed as non-native by Small - but as a native by WH

Galactia
"milk-pea"; *Galactia* spp.; Species undetermined, but due species may be *Galactia striata* (Jacq.) Urb., the only *Galactia* species described by WH as occupying coastal hammocks

Gallinule, Florida
Gallinula chloropus L. - common moorhen

Gallinule, Purple
Porphyrula martinica L.

Geobalanus
"gopher-apple"; *Licania michauxii* Prance

Geobalanus incana
"white-leaved gopher-apple"; *Licania michauxii* Prance

Geobalanus oblongifolius
"gopher-apple"; *Licania michauxii* Prance

Glycine apios
"groundnut"; *Apios americana* Medik.

Gordonia lasianthus
"loblolly-bay"; *Gordonia lasianthus* (L.) J. Ellis

Gossypium punctatum
"wild-cotton"; *Gossypium hirsutum* L.; listed as endangered by FDACS

green-turtle
Chelonia mydas

Groundsel-bush
Baccharis halimifolia L.

guava shrubs
likely *Psidium guajava* L., but potentially *P. cattleianum* Sabine; both listed as non-natives by WH

Guettarda scabra
"rough velvet-seed"; *Guettarda scabra* (L.) Vent.

Guilandina crista
"gray-nicker"; *Caesalpinia bonduc* (L.) Roxb.

Guzmannia
Guzmania monostachia (L.) Rusby ex Mez - West Indian tufted airplant; listed as endangered by FDACS

Hamamelis
"witch-hazel"; *Hamamelis virginiana* L. - America witchhazel

Hamelia
"fire-bush"; *Hamelia patens* Jacq.

***Harrisia,* three kinds in Florida**
Harrisia aboriginum Small ex Britton & Rose - prickly applecactus; *Harrisia fragrans* Small ex Britton & Rose - Indian River prickly-apple, listed as endangered by FDACS and USFWS; *Harrisia simpsonii* Small ex Britton & Rose - Simpson's applecactus

Heliotropium
"heliotrope"; likely *Heliotropium polyphyllum* Lehm.

Heliotropium leavenworthii
"yellow-heliotrope"; *Heliotropium polyphyllum* Lehm. - pineland heliotrope

Hickories
Carya spp.

Hicoria
"hickory"; likely *Carya glabra* (Mill.) Sweet - pignut hickory, but could potentially be *Carya alba* (L.) Nutt. - mockernut hickory

Hicoria glabra
"hickory"; *Carya glabra* (Mill.) Sweet - pignut hickory

Hieracium
"hawkweed"; *Hieracium* sp.

Hippomane mancinella
"manchineel"; *Hippomane mancinella* L.; listed as endangered by FDACS

Hymenocallis
"spider-lilys"; *Hymenocallis* spp. - Species undetermined.

Hypericum
"St. Johns Wort"; species undetermined - possible *Hypericum fasciculatum* Lam.

Hypericum fasciulatum
"yellow woody sand-weed", "sand-weed"; *Hypericum fasciculatum* Lam.

Ibidium
"ladies' tresses"; *Spiranthes* sp.

Ibidium cernuum
"ladies' tresses"; *Spiranthes odorata* (Nutt.) Lindl.

Ibidium laciniatum
"one white (orchid) and rather inconspicuous"; *Spiranthes laciniata* (Small) Ames - lacelip ladiestresses; synonym by J.K. Small, listed as threatened by FDACS

Icacorea
"marlberry"; likely *Ardisia escallonoides* Schiede & Deppe ex Schltdl. & Cham.

Icacorea paniculata
"wild-coffee", "marlberry"; *Ardisia escallonoides* Schiede & Deppe ex Schltdl. & Cham. - marlberry

Ichthyomethia
"Jamaica-dogwood"; *Piscidia piscipula* (L.) Sarg.

Ichthyomethia piscipula
"Jamaica-dogwood"; *Piscidia piscipula* (L.) Sarg.

Ilex cassine
"Dahoon", "Yaupon"; *Ilex cassine* L.

Ilex glabra
"gallberry"; *Ilex glabra* (L.) A. Gray

Ilex krugiana
"West Indian holly"; *Ilex krugiana* Loes.; listed as endangered by FDACS

Ilysanthes
"pimpernel"; Species undetermined, but possibly *Lindernia dubia* (L.) Pennell or *Lindernia grandiflora* Nutt.

Ipomoea
"real root which produces numerous herbaceous vines","ipomoea"; likely *Ipomoea macrorhiza* Michx - largeroot morning glory

Ipomoea macrorhiza
"ipomoea", "giant-rooted morning-glory"; *Ipomoea macrorhiza* Michx - largeroot morning glory; listed as an non-native by WH, but not Small

Ipomoea pandurata
"man-of-the-earth"; *Ipomoea pandurata* (L.) G. Mey.

Ipomoea pes-capri
"railroad-vine"; *Ipomoea pes-caprae* (L.) R. Br.

Iris
"blue-flags"; likely *Iris hexagona* Walter - prairie iris; this is the most widespread iris in Florida

Jacquinia keyensis
"Joe-wood"; *Jacquinia keyensis* Mez; listed as threatened by FDACS

Juncus
"rushes", *Juncus* spp.; species undetermined

Juncus roemerianus
"dark-green or brownish rush"; *Juncus roemerianus* Scheele - needle rush

Jussiaea
"evening-primrose"; *Ludwigia* spp.; species undetermined

Jussiaea peruviana
"Peruvian evening-primrose"; *Ludwigia peruviana* (L.) H. Hara; listed as non-native by WH

Koniga maritima
"sweet-alyssum"; *Lobularia maritima* (L.)Desv. ; listed as a non-native by WH and Small

Kosteletzkya althaeifolia
"mallow"; *Kosteletzkya virginica* (L.) C. Presl ex A. Gray

Laguncularia
"white mangrove"; *Laguncularia racemosa* (L.) C.F. Gaertn.

Lantana ovalitifolia
This name is a synonym of *Lantana depressa* Small, which is now only known from Miami-Dade County (and listed as endangered by FDACS). The species Small likely was referring to is *L. involucrata* L. - buttonsage, which occurs on coastal hammocks in the Halifax River region in which his reference location occurs.

Lasiacus
"wild-bamboo"; likely *Lasiacis divaricata* (L.) Hitchc.

Lemon tree
Citrus x limon (L.) Burm.

Leontodon
"dandelion", *Taraxacum officinale* Weber ex F.H. Wigg, common dandelion

Lepidium virginicum
"pepper-grass"; *Lepidium virginicum* L.

Leptoglottis
"sensitive-brier"; likely *Mimosa quadrivalvis* L.

Lcttucc
Lactuca sativa L.

Leucothoë
"fetterbush"; likely either *Leucothoe axillaris* (Lam.) D. Don - coastal doghobble or *Leucothoe racemosa* (L.) A. Gray - swamp doghobble

lilac
Syringa vulgaris L.

Limodorum
"grass pink"; *Calopogon* sp.

Live-oak
Quercus virginiana Mill.

Long-leaf pine
Pinus palustris Mill.

Lygodesmia aphylla
"pine-pink"; *Lygodesmia aphylla* (Nutt.) DC.

Lysiloma bahamensis
"wild-tamarind"; *Lysiloma latisiliquum* (L.) Benth.

Magnolia
"sweet-bay"; *Magnolia virginiana* L.

Magnolia foetida
"magnolia", "big-magnolia"; *Magnolia grandiflora* L.

Magnolia virginiana
"sweet-bay"; *Magnolia virginiana* L.

Mangrove, Black
Avicennia germinans (L.) L.

Mangrove, Button
Conocarpus erectus L. - buttonwood

Mangrove, Red
Rhizophora mangle L.

Mangrove, the four different kinds
Avicennia germinans (L.) L. - black mangrove, *Conocarpus erectus* L. - buttonwood or button mangrove, *Rhizophora mangle* L. - red mangrove, and *Laguncularia racemosa* (L.) C.F. Gaertn. - white mangrove

Mangrove, White
Laguncularia racemosa (L.) C.F. Gaertn.

maples
Acer spp.

Mariscus jamaicensis
"sedge"; *Cladium jamaicense* Crantz - sawgrass

Mentzelia
"poor-man's patches"; *Mentzelia floridana* Nutt. Ex Torr. & A. Gray

Metastelma blodgettii
"milkweed"; *Cynanchum blodgettii* (A. Gray) Shinners; listed as threatened by FDACS

Metopium
"poison-wood"; *Metopium toxiferum* (L.) Krug & Urb.

Metopium metopium
"poison-wood"; *Metopium toxiferum* (L.) Krug & Urb.

Mimusops
"wild-dilly"; *Manilkara jaimiqui* (C. Wright ex Griseb.) Dubard; listed as threatened by FDACS

Misanteca triandra
Licaria triandra (Sw.) Kosterm. - pepperleaf sweetwood; listed as endangered by FDACS; currently only known from one park in Dade County

Momisia
"chaparral-shrub"; likely *Celtis iguanaea* (Jacq.) Sarg., but possibly *C. ehrenbergiana* (Klotzsch) Liebm.; Both species are listed as endangered by FDACS

Momordica balsamea
"balsam-apple"; *Momordica balsamina* L.; listed as non-native by WH and Small

Moon-flower
possibly *Ipomoea alba* L.

Morinda roioc
"cheese-shrub"; *Morinda royoc* L. - redgal

Morus
"mulberry trees"; *Morus rubra* L.

Morus rubra
"mulberry"; *Morus rubra* L.

Muscadini
"muscadine-grape"; *Vitis rotundifolia* Michx.

Muscadinia munsniana
"wild-muscadine"; *Vitis rotundifolia* Michx.

Needle-palm
Rhapidophyllum hystrix (Pursh.) H. Wendl. & Drude ex Drude; listed as commercially exploited by FDACS

Neopieris mariana
"lambkill"; *Lyonia mariana* (L.) D. Don - Piedmont staggerbush

Neowashingtonia robusta
"Washington palm"; *Washingtonia robusta* H.Wendl.; listed as a non-native by WH

Nephrolepis
"Boston-fern"; likely *Nephrolepis exaltata* (L.) Schott

Nephrolepis exaltata
"Boston-fern"; *Nephrolepis exaltata* (L.) Schott

Nintooa japonica
"Japanese honeysuckle"; *Lonicera japonica* Thunb.; listed as non-native by WH

Nymphaea macrophylla
"spatterdock"; *Nuphar advena* (Aiton) W.T. Aiton

Ocimum micranthum
"mosquito-plant"; *Ocimum campechianum* Mill.; listed as endangered by FDACS

Oncidium floridanum
Oncidium ensatum Lindl. - Florida dancinglady orchid; listed as endangered by FDACS

Opuntia
"prickly pear"; likely *Opuntia humifusa* (Raf.) Raf.

Opuntia eburnispina
"something different from that of our other known species of Opuntia"; *Opuntia humifusa* (Raf.) Raf.

Opuntia abjecta
Opuntia triacanthos (Willd.) Sweet - keys joe-jumper; listed as endangered by FDACS

Opuntia dillenii
Opuntia stricta (Haw.) Haw.; listed as threatened by FDACS

Opuntia ficus-indica
"spineless cactus"; *Opuntia ficus-indica* (L.) Mill.; listed as not-native by WH, Small's notation of this species within the "lime-sink region" north of Hernando County would represent an extension to the known range of the species (currently only known from Escambia County in the panhandle)

Opuntia ochrocentra
"(cactus with) longer and relatively more slender straight spines"; *Opuntia cubensis* Britton & Rose; this notation by Small represents an extension to the known range of the species (from the Keys)

Opuntia polycarpa
"prickly-pear"; *Opuntia humifusa* (Raf.) Raf.

Opuntia zebrina
"striped-spined prickly-pear"; *Opuntia stricta* (Haw.) Haw.; listed as threatened by FDACS

Opuntiae
"prickly-pears"; various species of cactus including *Opuntia stricta* (Haw.) Haw. and *Opuntia cubensis* Britton & Rose

orange tree
Citrus x aurantium L.

Orontium
"golden-club"; *Orontium aquaticum* L. - goldenclub, neverwet

oysters
Cassostrea virginica Gmelin

Padus virginiana
"choke-cherry"; *Prunus serotina* Ehrh.

Panicum bartowense
"panic-grass"; *Panicum dichotomiflorum* var. bartowense (Scribn. & Merr.) Fernald

Parthenocissus quinquefolia
"Virginia-creeper"; *Parthenocissus quinquefolia* (L.) Planch.

Passiflora incarnata
"may-pop"; *Passiflora incarnata* L. - purple passionflower

Paurotis wrightii
"saw-cabbage palm"; *Acoelorraphe wrightii* (Griseb. & H. Wendl.) H. Wendl. ex Becc. - everglades palm; listed as threatened by FDACS

Pear
Pyris communis L.

Peperomia cummulicola
"wild-pepper plant"; *Peperomia humilis* A. Dietr. - low peperomia; listed as endangered by FDACS

Peperomia humilis
"wild-pepper plant"; *Peperomia humilis* A. Dietr. - low peperomia; listed as endangered by FDACS

Peperomia spathulifolia
"wild-pepper"; *Peperomia magnoliifolia* (Jacq.) A. Dietr. - spoonleaf peperomia; listed as endangered by FDACS

Peppers
likely *Capsicum annuum* L.

Pereskia pereskia
"Barbados-gooseberry"; *Pereskia aculeata* Mill.; listed as non-native by WH and Small

Persicaria
"smart-weed"; Polygonum spp.; Species undetermined.

Petiveria
"skunk-bush"; *Petiveria alliacea* L.

Phlebodium
"serpent-fern"; *Phlebodium aureum* (L.) J. Sm.

Phlox amoena
"very brilliant phlox"; *Phlox amoena* Sims - hairy phlox

Phlox drummondii
"phlox"; *Phlox drummondii* Hook. - annual phlox; listed as non-native by Small and WH

Phyllanthus speciousus
Species undetermined

Phymatodes exigua
"vine-fern"; *Microgramma heterophylla* (L.) Wherry; listed as endangered by FDACS; Although still rare, this species is now known to occur in more locations than reported by Small.

Phytolacca rigida
"pokeweed"; *Phytolacca americana* L.

Piaropus crassipes
"water-hyacinth"; *Eichornia crassipes* (Mart.) Solms; listed as non-native by WH

Picea abies
"Norway spruce"; *Picea abies* (L.) Karst

Pinus clausa
"spruce pine"; *Pinus clausa* (Chapm. Ex Engelm.) Vasey ex Sarg. - sand pine

Piriquita
"golden-saucers"; *Piriqueta cistoides* (L.) Griseb. - pitted stripeseed

Pisonia
"devil's claws"; likely *Pisonia aculeata* L.

Pisonia aculeata
"devil's claws"; *Pisonia aculeata* L.

Pistia
"water-lettuce"; *Pistia stratiotes* L.

Pitcher-plants
Sarracenia spp. - likely *Sarracenia flava* L. in the north and *Sarracenia minor* Walter in the south

Pithecolobium
"cat's-claw" likely refers to *Pithecellobium unguis-cati* (L.) Benth., while "black-bead" refers to either cat's claw or possibly P. *keyense* Britton ex Britton & Rose; the latter species is listed as threatened by FDACS

Pithecolobium unguis-cati
"cat's-claw"; *Pithecellobium unguis-cati* (L.) Benth.

Pluchea
"marsh-fleabane"; *Pluchea* spp. - Species undetermined

Pluchea odorata
"tropical flea-bane"; *Pluchea odorata* (L.) Cass.; Small notes that this species appears to have spread into peninsular Florida from Key West, but WH notes this as a native species.

Podophyllum
"may-apple"; *Podophyllum peltatum* L.

Pogonia ophioglossoides
"snake-mouth"; *Pogonia ophioglossoides* (L.) R. Br.

Polygala
"yellow bachelor's-button"; the yellow polygala could refer to *Polygala cymosa* Walter, *Polygala ramosa* Elliott, or *Polygala rugelii* Shuttlew. ex Chapm.

Polygala cymosa
"yellow milkwort"; *Polygala cymosa* Walter - high pinebarren milkwort

Polygala ramosa
"yellow milkwort"; *Polygala ramosa* Elliott - low pinebarren milkwort

Polygala lutea
"yellow milkwort"; *Polygala lutea* L. - orange milkwort

Polyrrhiza lindenii
"Cuban orchid"; *Dendrophylax lindenii* (Lindl.) Benth. ex Rolfe - ghost orchid; listed as endangered by FDACS; subject of the book The Orchid Thief, s. Orlean. 1998. Random House"

Polystachya
refers to *Polystachya concreta* (Jacq.) Garay & H.R. Sweet - greater yellowspike orchid; listed as endangered by FDACS

Pontederia
"pickerel-weed", "wampee"; *Pontederia cordata* L.

Pontederia cordata
"pickerel-weed", "wampee"; *Pontederia cordata* L.

Prunus
"wild plum"; likely *Prunus americana* Marshall - American plum

Pseudophoenix vinifera
"buccaneer-palms"; *Pseudophoenix sargentii* H. Wendl. ex Sarg.; listed as endangered by FDACS

Psidium guajava
"guava"; *Psidium guajava* L.; listed as non-native by WH

Psilotum nudum
"whisp-fern"; *Psilotum nudum* (L.) P.Beauv. - whisk-fern

Psychotria
"wild-coffee"; likely either *Psychotria nervosa* Sw. or *P. sulzneri* Small

Psychotria sulzneri
"wild-coffee"; *Psychotria sulzneri* Small; species described by Small

Psychotria undata
"wild-coffee"; *Psychotria nervosa* Sw.

Pterocaulon
"black-root"; *Pterocaulon pycnostachyum* (Michx.) Elliott

Quercus catesbaei
"turkey-oak", "black-jack"; *Quercus laevis* Walter. - turkey oak

Quercus cinerea
"upland willow-oak"; *Quercus incana* W. Bartram - bluejack oak

Quercus nigra
"water-oak"; *Quercus nigra* L.

Quercus rubra
referred to as "pin oak", likely *Quercus rubra* L. - northern red oak because of distribution ("in the north") versus the pin oak *(Quercus palustris* Muenchh.) that is limited in distribution in New York

Quercus virginiana
"live-oak"; *Quercus virginiana* Mill.

Raccoon
Procyon lotor

Randia
"box-brier"; *Randia aculeata* L. - white indigoberry

Randia aculeata
"box-brier"; *Randia aculeata* L. - white indigoberry

Rapanea
"myrsine"; likely *Rapanea punctata* (Lam.) Lundell

Rapanea guianensis
"myrsine"; *Rapanea punctata* (Lam.) Lundell

Red-cedar
Juniperus virginiana L. - red cedar

Reynosia septentronalis
"darling-plum"; *Reynosia septentrionalis* Urb.

Rhizophora mangle
"red-mangrove"; *Rhizophora mangle* L.

Rhododendron chapmanii
"Chapman-honeysuckle"; *Rhododendron minus* Michx. Var. *chapmanii* (A. Gray) W.H. Duncan & Pullen; listed as endangered by FDACS and the USFWS

Ricinus communis
"castor-bean"; *Ricinus communis* L.; listed as non-native by WH

Roystonea regia
"royal-palm"; *Roystonea regia* (Kunth) O.F. Cook; listed as endangered by FDACS

Rubus
"sand-blackberry"; *Rubus* spp.

Ruellia parviflora
"rose-pink ruellia"; *Ruellia caroliniensis* (J.F. Gmel.) Steud.

Sabal
"cabbage-trees"; *Sabal palmetto* (Walter) Lodd. Ex Schult. & Schult. - cabbage palm

Sabal minor
"dwarf-palmetto"; *Sabal minor* (Jacq.) Pers.

Sabbatia
"marsh pink"; *Sabatia* sp.

Sabina silicicola
"red-cedar"; *Juniperus virginiana* L.

Sageretia minutiflora
"spiny buckthorn"; *Sageretia minutiflora* (Michx) C. Mohr

Sagittaria
"arrowheads"; Species undetermined.

Sagittaria lancifolia
"giant arrow-head"; *Sagittaria lancifolia* L.

Salicornia ambigua
"samphire"; *Sarcocornia perennis* (Mill.) A.J. Scott

Salix
"willow"; likely *Salix caroliniana* Michx.

Salvia
Salvia spp.

Salvia coccinea
"scarlet sage"; *Salvia coccinea* Buc'hoz ex Etl.

salvia, salvias
Salvia spp.

Sambucus
"elder trees"; *Sambucus nigra* L., the appropriate name for the more commonly used synonym *Sambucus canadensis* L.

Sambucus simpsonii
"elder"; *Sambucus nigra* L., the appropriate name for the more commonly used synonym *Sambucus canadensis* L.

Sapindus
"soapberry"; *Sapindus saponaria* L.

Sapindus marginatus
"soapberry"; *Sapindus saponaria* L.

Sapindus saponaria
"soapberry"; *Sapindus saponaria* L.

Sarracenia
"pitcher-plant"; likely *Sarracenia minor* Walter - hooded pitcher plant

Sarracenia minor
"small pitcher plant"; *Sarracenia minor* Walter - hooded pitcher plant; listed as threatened by FDACS

Saururus
"lizard's-tail"; *Saururus cernuus* L.

Savia bahamensis
"savia"; *Savia bahamensis* Britton - Bahama maidenbush; listed as endangered by FDACS; Florida distribution is solely in the Keys

Scaevola plumieri
"shrub-lobelia"; *Scaevola plumieri* (L.) Vahl - beachberry; listed as threatened by FDACS

Scarlet-sage
likely *Salvia coccinea* Buc'hoz ex Etl.

Scirpus validus
"bulrush"; *Scirpus tabernaemontani* C.C. Gmel.

Scrub-oak *(Quercus)*
the description of this scrub oak on a dune suggests that it is likely *Quercus myrtifolia* Willd. - myrtle oak, although Small may have been referring to *Quercus geminata* Small - sand live oak

Senecio
"ragworts"

Senecio lobatus
"ragwort"; *Packera glabella* (Poir.) C. Jeffrey - butterweed

Serenoa
"saw-palmetto"; *Serenoa repens* (W. Bartram) Small; current scientific name originated by Small

Serenoa repens
"saw-palmetto"; *Serenoa repens* (W. Bartram) Small; current scientific name originated by Small

Sesuvium portulacastrum
"sea-purslane"; *Sesuvium portulacastrum* (L.) L.

Pine, short-leaf in the scrub
Pinus clausa (Chapm. ex Engelm.) Vasey ex Sarg. - sand pine

Sideroxylon
"mastic"; likely *Sideroxylon foetidissimum* Jacq.

Sideroxylon mastichodendrom
"mastic"; *Sideroxylon foetidissimum* Jacq.

Simaruba glauca
"paradise-tree"; *Simaruba glauca* DC.

Sitilias caroliniana
"lemon-drops"; *Pyrrhopappus carolinianus* (Walter) DC. - desert chicory

Slash-pine
Pinus elliottii Engelm.

Smilax
"bamboos", "greenbriers", "china-brief"; *Smilax* - species undetermined

Smilax beyrichii
"cat-brier"; *Smilax auriculata* Walter

Solanum
"cankerberry"; possibly *Solanum bahamense* L.

Solanum blodgettii
"Blodgett-potato"; *Solanum donianum* Walp. - mullein nightshade

Solanum torvum
"bushy potato"; *Solanum torvum* Sw.; listed as non-native by WH and Small

Solidago
"goldenrod"; Undetermined species.

Sonchus oleraceus
"sow-thistle"; *Sonchus oleraceus* L.; listed as non-native by WH

Spartina
"switch-grass"; likely *Spartina bakeri* Merr. - sand cordgrass

Spartina bakeri
"switch-grass"; *Spartina bakeri* Merr. - sand cordgrass

Spathiger
likely *Epidendrum rigidum* Jacq. - rigid epidendrum; listed as endangered by FDACS

Spathyema
"skunk cabbage"; *Symplocarpus foetidus* (L.) Salisb. ex Nutt.

Sphenomeris clavata
"little West Indian fern"; *Odontosoria clavata* (L.) J.Sm.

Stillingia
"queen's-root"; *Stillingia sylvatica* L.

Stillingia spathulata
"queen's-delight"; *Stillingia sylvatica* L.

Stomoisia juncea
"yellow bladderwort"; *Utricularia juncea* Vahl

Suriana
"bay-cedar"; *Suriana maritima* L.

Suriana maritime
"bay-cedar"; *Suriana maritima* L.

Talisia pedicillaris
Talisia pedicillaris Radlk. - black moraballi; the USF Plant Atlas does not include this species in the Flora of Florida - Small notes as a rarity in Florida

Tamala
"red-bays"; likely *Persea borbonia* (L.) Spreng. - red bay

Tamala pubescens
"swamp-bay"; *Persea palustris* (Raf.) Sarg.

Taxodium
"cypress"; likely *Taxodium distichum* (L.) Rich.

Taxodium distichum
"cypress"; *Taxodium distichum* (L.) Rich.

Tectaria
"four kinds of halberd-fern"; likely *Tectaria coriandrifolia* (Sw.) Underw., *T. fimbriata* (Willd.) Proctor & Lourteig, *T. heracleifolia* (Willd.) Underw., and possibly *T. incisa* Cav.. The first two species are listed as endangered by FDACS, the third species as threatened by FDACS, and the last is now considered an exotic by WH

Tectaria minima
"small halberd-fern"; *Tectaria fimbriata* (Willd.) Proctor & Lourteig; listed as endangered by FDACS

Teucrium
"germander"; *Teucrium canadense* L.

Thrimax parviflora
"thatch-palm"; *Thrinax radiata* Lodd. Ex Schult. & Schult. f.; listed as endangered by FDACS

Thunbergia alta
"thunbergia"; *Thunbergia alata* Bojer ex Sims - blackeyed susan vine; listed as exotic by WH and Small

Thunbergia fragrans
"thunbergia"; *Thunbergia fragrans* Roxb. - whitelady; listed as exotic by WH and Small

Tilia heterophylla
"linden"; *Tilia americana* L. - basswood

Tillandsia
"wild pine"; *Tillandsia* spp. - Species undetermined

Tournefortia
"heliotrope-vine"; likely *Tournefortia volubilis* L.

Tournefortia gnaphaloides
"beach-heliotrope"; *Argusia gnaphalodes* (L.) Heine - sea rosemary; listed as endangered by FDACS

Tournefortia poliochros
"heliotrope-vine"; *Tournefortia volubilis* L.

Tracyanthus
"fly-poison"; *Stenanthium densum* (Desr.) Zomlefer & Judd - crowpoison; synonym of *Zigadenus densus* (Desr.) Fernald

Tradescantella floridana
"little spiderwort"; *Callisia cordifolia* (Sw.) E.S. Anderson & Woodson - Florida roseling

Trailing arbutus
Epigaea repens L.

Tricholaena
"natalgrass"; *Rhynchelytrum repens* (Willd.) C.E. Hubb; listed as an nonnative by Small and WH

Trichomanes krausii
"filmy-fern"; *Trichomanes krausii* Hook. & Grev. - Kraus' bristle fern; listed as endangered by FDACS

Trichomanes punctata
"a fan-shaped filmy one (fern)"; *Trichomanes punctatum* Poir. - Florida bristle fern; listed as endangered by FDACS

Tripsacum
"gamma-grass"; likely *Tripsacum dactyloides* (L.) L. - Fakahatcheegrass

Tubiflora angustifolia
"chaff-acanthus"; *Elytraria caroliniensis* (J.F. Gmel.) Pers. var. angustifolia (Fernald) S.F. Blake

Typha
"cat-tail"; either *Typha domingensis* Pers. or *Typha latifolia* L.

Verbena polystachya
"vervain"; *Verbena polystachya* Humb., Bonpl. & Kunth; WH does not include this species as part of the Florida flora; this species is a cultivated species

Verbena maritima
"dune-verbena"; *Glandularia maritima* (Small) Small; species described by Small. Small notes this species as being a species of "prominence", but this species is now listed as endangered by FDACS.

Vernonia altissima
"iron-weed"; *Vernonia gigantea* (Walter) Trel. ex Branner & Coville

Viburnum
"with-rod"; likely *Viburnum nudum* L.

Viola
"violets"

Viola pedata
"birds-foot violet"; *Viola pedata* L.

Viorna baldwinii
"pine-hyacinth"; *Clematis baldwinii* Torr. & A. Gray

Vitis
"grape"; likely *Vitis rotundifolia* Michx. - muscadine or *Vitis aestivalis* Michx. - summer grape

Vitis aestivalis
"grape"; *Vitis aestivalis* Michx.

Vitis cinerea
"grape"; *Vitis cinerea* (Engelm.) Engelm. ex Millardet

Walnut
likely *Juglans nigra* L. - black walnut

Water-hyacinth
Eichhornia crassipes (Mart.) Solms; listed as non-native by WH

Xanthium
"clotbur"; *Xanthium strumarium* L. - cockleburr

Ximenesia encelioides
"golden crownbeard"; *Verbesina encelioides* (Cav.) Benth & Hook. F. ex A. Gray; listed as non-native by Small and WH

Ximenia
"hog-plum"; *Ximenia americana* L.

Ximenia americana
"hog-plum"; *Ximenia americana* L.

Yellow-bell
likely *Tecoma stans* (L.) Juss. ex Kunth

Yucca
"Spanish bayonet"; likely *Yucca aloifolia* L.

Yucca aloifolia
"Spanish bayonet"; *Yucca aloifolia* L.

Yucca filamentosa
"bear-grass"; *Yucca filamentosa* L.

Zamia
"coontie", "conti", "native zamia"; *Zamia pumila* L.

Zanthoxylum
"toothache-tree"; likely *Zanthoxylum clava-herculis* L. - hercule's club

Zanthoxylum clava-herculis
"cool-and-easy", "toothache-tree"; *Zanthoxylum clava-herculis* L.

Zanthoxylum fagara
"wild lime"; *Zanthoxylum fagara* (L.) Sarg.

Bibliography

Wunderlin, R.P., and B.F. Hansen. 2003. *Guide to the Vascular Plants of Florida,* Second Edition. University Press of Florida, Gainesville, FL.

Brown, P.M. 2002. *Wild Orchids of Florida.* University Press of Florida, Gainesville, FL

Chafin, L.G. 2000. *Field Guide to the Rare Plants of Florida.* Florida Natural Areas Inventory, Tallahassee, Florida

Wunderlin, R. P., and B. F. Hansen. 2004. *Atlas of Florida Vascular Plants* (http://www.plantatlas.usf.edu/).[S. M. Landry and K. N. Campbell (application development), Florida Center for Community Design and Research.] Institute for Systematic Botany, University of South Florida, Tampa.

USDA, NRCS. 2004. The PLANTS Database, Version 3.5 (http://plants.usda.gov). National Plant Data Center, Baton Rouge, LA 70874-4490 USA

Envirotools - Tess 2.0 - version 2000.

Notes

1 *Journey of Alvar Nuñez Cabeza de Vaca.* Translation by Ad. F. Bandelier. 1905

2 The hammock—the word probably of Indian origin—is a dense growth of mostly broad-leaved trees and shrubs. Sometimes hammock growth occupies a whole geologic formation, at other times it exists as islands, so to speak, in pinewoods or on prairies, or surrounded by other plant associations. They occur only in regions protected from fire, or in fire-ravaged regions they represent areas that fire has not yet run through. It cannot be correlated with altitude or with soil, for beneath the humus, resulting from the decaying vegetable matter, may be sand, clay, marl, or rock. The use of the word is confined mostly to Florida and adjacent States.

3 The pinewoods or pinelands of Florida are nearly level areas of greater or less extent; the high pinelands are dry and often somewhat rolling; the low pinelands where the water-table is always near the surface are often called "flatwoods" because of the flatness of the land. They are composed, according to locality or region, of one or another of the several long-leaved pines. The undergrowth consists of saw-palmetto, shrubs (particularly scrub-oaks), and annual and perennial herbs. They are often fire-swept, and consequently the soil, sand or rock floor, is nearly or quite devoid of humus. As a result of frequent fires and an impoverished soil, there is no tall growth aside from the pine trees which do not require humus as do broad-leaved trees.

4 This and the following high mounds have been named by Mrs. Peckham from evident characters associated with each mound.

5 This kitchen-midden has been completely destroyed.

6 The scrub is a plant association typified by a growth of spruce pine *(Pinus clausa),* evergreen scrub-oaks, Florida-rosemary, and a number of endemic shrubs and herbs. These areas of white sand varying from a few square yards to many acres in extent, range from northern Florida southward on the western coast to Marco Island and on the eastern coast to Miami.

7 The black-jack ridges comprise large areas in Florida. They are

irregular in shape and placement or in parallel ranges. They are dry and rather barren. Oaks, black-jack *(Quercus catesbaei)* and upland willow-oak *(Q. cinerea),* often called black-jack, are the most conspicuous broad-leaved trees.

8 *Journal of the New York Botanical Garden* 24: 11. 1923.

9 The lake region comprises a large area on the backbone of the State. The surface is very hilly. Some of the hills are steep and some rise to over two hundred feet above the sea. Between them are thousands of small round lakes or large irregular lakes. The soil is sand which is often snow-white and frequently supports large areas of vegetation called "scrub."

10 The lime-sink region, extending as an irregular area somewhat diagonally from Hernando County up into southern Georgia, is largely rolling sandy pine woods with many depressions or sinks. There are a few streams. The depressions are mostly dry in the northern parts. Further south they often contain water. Springs are frequent along the few rivers.

11 The Gulf Hammock region extends along the coast from Tarpon Springs to Saint Marks. Inland it covers from fifteen to twenty miles and has little altitude. It contains many low hammocks, some of which, especially the great Gulf Hammock, are large in extent and comprise a considerable number of different kinds of broad-leaved trees.

12 *Journal of the New York Botanical Garden* 25: 62, 63. 1924.

13 *Journal of the New York Botanical Garden* 25:63. 1924.

14 *Journal of the New York Botanical Garden* 22: 121–137. 1921.

15 The aborigines, the Creeks (Seminoles), and the white man have all drawn on the natural supply of plants for starch or flour. Today a certain cracker of one of our large biscuit companies is made from flour derived from the wild zamias of Florida.

16 There are several dozen very interesting shell-mounds in the upper (southern) reaches of Salt River and over in Homosassa River and Saint Martin's River. Some mounds are built up on the shores of the streams and lagoons; others on rock reefs in the waters. The latter showing banks of weathered white or gray shells capped by the greenery of various shrubs and trees are exceedingly picturesque objects rising from the green or blue water.

17 *Journal of the New York Botanical Garden* 21: 34–38. 1920.

18 *Journal of the New York Botanical Garden* 25: 66, 67. 1924

19 The Everglade Keys or the Miami Limestone Region, an area of exposed oölitic limestone, consists of a chain of islands enclosed by the southern portion of the Everglades, except where some of the islands come in contact with the upper half of Bay Biscayne. The chain stretches, in crescent form, from somewhat north of the Miami River southwestward toward Cape Sable for a distance of about fifty-five miles. The islands, apparently, in ancient times formed a part of the Antilles. This was when the subterranean mountain whose summit makes the present peninsula of Florida was less elevated. The native vegetation of the islands is essentially of a tropical character, with strong relationships to the flora of Cuba and of the Bahamas. As far as the native flora is concerned the Everglade Keys represent a small tropical area isolated on the mainland of the United States. There are two main divisions, the Biscayne Pineland and the Long-Pine Key Pineland.

20 This hammock, and more than a score similar to it, are associations of tropical shrubs and trees in the pinelands of the Everglade Keys. The trees are mostly those widely distributed in the West Indies. However, there are several rarities, for example, one—*Misanteca triandra*—of Cuba and Jamaica and another—*Talisia pedicillaris*—which is otherwise not known this side of British Guiana. There are two woody tropical plant-associations in Florida, the one just referred to and the maritime one consisting of the mangroves and associated trees and shrubs.

21 Cape Sable, Florida, comprising three capes—East, Middle, and Northwest—is a crescent-shaped plateau built up of marl and sand. It is slightly elevated above high tide. Vast prairies which dominate support scattered hammocks of tropical trees and shrubs. It is bounded on the east by mangrove swamps and on the north by White Water Bay and the Ten Thousand Islands. The East Cape is the most southern point on the mainland of the United States. Key West lies about sixty miles to the southwest.

22 This is a branch highway running three miles to the settlement of Flamingo on Florida Bay. It is named for Stephen J. Roberts, long a resident of Flamingo.

23 Hungry Land; so called, it is said, because a herd of stolen cattle were there penned up and allowed to starve, when the frightened

thieves fled. It is a desolate and uninhabited region lying between Jupiter and the Allapattah Flats. It is characterized by cypress swamps and flat-woods.

24 The Saint Lucie Slough is a stretch of low country between Lake Okeechobee and the headwaters of the Saint Lucie River. The fifth water-highway leading out of Lake Okeechobee to the Saint Lucie River near the eastern coast has been dredged through that region.

25 *Journal of the New York Botanical Garden* 19:279–290. 1918. *Journal of the American Museum of Natural History* 18: 685–700. 1918.

26 Royal-Palm hammocks back of Marco Island consist of two separated groups of palm trees. Originally there were numerous palms in each colony, but the wholesale removal of trees for ornamental plantings at distant points and the cutting down of many individuals for securing seeds for planting has greatly depleted the original growth.

27 See *Journal of the New York Botanical Garden* 23: 142–144. 1922; 24: 227–229. 1923

28 *Journal of the New York Botanical Garden* 25: 237–244. 1924

29 This plant has been described as *Opuntia eburnispina,* Small, Britton and Rose, *The Cactaceae* 4: 260. 1924. The specific name refers to the ivory white spines.

30 The southern half of peninsular Florida has several large prairies, besides the Everglades which comprise some three hundred thousand acres. The Everglades including Lake Okeechobee are wet prairies, essentially a lake in the rainy season (summer), and partly dry in the dry season (winter). To the west of the Everglades south of the Caloosahatchee is the Big Cypress swamp with extensive prairies and north of the Caloosahatchee lies the Indian prairie. North of the Everglades are the Lake Istokpaga prairies, the Kissimmee prairies, and the Okeechobee prairies. The elevation of the land or average water-table is evidently responsible for the nearly treeless condition, for trees are found on small areas which are just a little higher than the vast expanse of the prairies. A few inches or a few feet elevation make a great difference in the vegetation.

31 *Journal of the New York Botanical Garden* 15: 69–79. 1914; 19: 279–290. 1918. *Journal of the American Museum of Natural History* 18: 684–700. 1918.

32 *Journal of the New York Botanical Garden* 22: 39. 1921.

33 Translation of a Memoir by Fontaneda by Buckingham Smith 15. 1854.

34 Long key is one of the upper Florida Keys of which there are nearly one hundred named on the charts. They extend from Soldier Key to near Bahia Honda Channel on the continental shelf. They are the remains of one of the later rock formations—the Key Largo Limestone which is largely an unchanged coral mass. They have been much weathered since they were elevated above the sea.

35 For a history of this palm see *Journal of the New York Botanical Garden* 23: 33–43. 1922.

36 Big Pine Key is the largest island of the lower Florida Keys of which there are more than one hundred named on the charts. They extend on the Continental shelf from near the Bahia Honda Channel to Key West. They are mostly the remains of a rock formation older than Key Largo Limestone—an oölitic limestone. The formation has been much broken down and sculptured since it was raised above the sea.

37 *Journal of the New York Botanical Garden* 22: 61, 62. 1921.

38 See *Journal of the New York Botanical Garden* 22: 200, 201. 1921.

39 *Journal of the New York Botanical Garden* 25: 76. 1924.

40 *Journal of the New York Botanical Garden* 18: 106. 1917.

41 *Journal of the New York Botanical Garden* 22: 50–53. 1921. 24: 212–214. 1923. 25: 75–79. 1924.

42 There was much aboriginal activity about Bay Biscayne. There were small village sites, kitchen-middens, and burial mounds similar to the one just referred to on the eastern side of the bay even on the islands—Virginia and Key Bay Biscayne. The large settlements, however, were on the mainland, especially about the mouths of streams. The larger ones seem to have been near the mouth of Arch Creek, the Miami River, and at Cutler, where there were numerous springs of water which came through subterranean channels from the Everglades. The present site of Miami was formerly an Indian village called Tequesta, as recorded by Hernando de Escalante Fontaneda—a prisoner in Florida for seventeen years—early in the sixteenth century. "The Martires [Florida Keys] end near a village of Indians called Tequesta, situated on the bank

of a river [Miami River] which comes from the interior of the country the distance of fifteen leagues, and issues from another lake of fresh water, which is said by some Indians, who have traversed it more than I, to be an arm of the Lake of Mayaimi [Lake Okeechobee]."

43 *The Journey of Alvar Nuñez Cabeza de Vaca.* Translation by A. F. Bandelier 66. 1905.

44 The aboriginal relic now lies under several feet of marl and sand pumped up from the bottom of Indian Creek, as shown in one of the accompanying plates.

45 *Journal of the New York Botanical Garden* 23: 154. 1922.

46 *Journal of the New York Botanical Garden* 25: pl. 285. 1924.

Index

Contributors to the New Edition

Jay Exum received his Ph.D. in wildlife ecology from Auburn University in 1985. Since that time, Dr. Exum has conducted vegetation and wildlife assessments on thousands of acres throughout Florida and the Southeast. He is particularly interested in evaluating and mitigating the impacts of man on natural systems in Florida, and he works with numerous public and private clients to minimize the effects of growth on natural systems in the state.

Randy Mejeur received his M.S. in botany from the University of Georgia in 1998, where his research interests focused on fire ecology, restoration ecology, and botanical explorations of the longleaf pine ecosystem. In his work as a botanist for an environmental consulting firm since 1998, Mr. Mejeur has conducted floral and faunal surveys on a variety of public and private lands, conducted wetland assessments throughout Florida, and developed management plans on conservation lands for the protection of rare species and restoration of natural systems. He continues to pursue innovative solutions to protect significant natural resources within a context of rapid urbanization as an Associate Ecologist at Glatting Jackson in Orlando, Florida.

Bill Belleville is an author and documentary filmmaker specializing in environmental issues. He has written over 1,000 non-fiction magazine articles and essays for such publications as *Newsweek, New York Times Syndicate, Audubon, Sierra, Sports Afield, Islands* and many others. His four books include the critically acclaimed *River of Lakes: A Journey on Florida's St. Johns River* (University of Georgia Press), which the *Miami Herald* described as the "definitive book" on this river system. He has also worked as a writer for the Discovery Channel on expeditions overseas, and won an Emmy award for producing and scripting "Wekiva: Legacy or Loss?" He has been named Environmental Writer of the Year by the Florida Audubon Society and the Florida Wildlife Federation. He has been Writer-in-Residence at the University of South Florida for the fall and spring semesters of 2004-2005. Mr. Belleville is also co-founder of Equinox Documentaries, Inc., a 501.c.3 dedicated to environmental education.

The Seminole Soil and Water Conservation District's mission is to promote natural resource conservation and education for land users and water consumers. To this end, we support the best land and water use management practices that conserve, improve, and sustain the natural environment of Seminole County.

The SSWCD was organized by landowners in Seminole County, Florida in 1947 under the Soil and Water Conservation Law, Chapter 582, Florida Statutes to assist the local landowners and users in making the best use of our natural resources. The district evolved out of an original mandate by U.S. President Franklin D. Roosevelt who sent a model law to all the states encouraging them to grant authority to farmers and ranchers to organize soil conservation districts. The president's concern was in direct response to the widespread erosion associated with the "Dust Bowl" of the Plains of the 1930's. Poor agricultural practices and years of sustained drought caused the Dust Bowl.

Aside from land management practices, general education and record keeping, our primary function is to seek the best policy for the future of Seminole County in regard to land and water use. Research and community involvement are our strongest conduits to the community's needs and expectations. As with other districts throughout the state, we act as a liaison between government agencies, private organizations, and the public at large.